THE LADDER OF TRUST

PRESS

Messianic Foundations:

Volume One
The Ladder of Trust

RON WARREN

TORAHLIFE PUBLISHING

**931 North State Road 434, Suite 1211-347,
Altamonte Springs, Fl. 32714.
PHONE (407) 443-5068**

www.xulonpress.com

Dedication

———⟨०/०⟩———

To God, who carried me, and loved me while I was rejecting, and hating Him and who brought me back to Himself through His grace and mercy, thus proving that He is the "God of a second chance."

To my wife, JoAnn, whose has proven her devotion and dedication to me at many stages through our passage of time together and our many struggles. Your ability to embrace my deepest needs and to accept the challenge of investing in the potential of my God given and anointed destiny has overwhelmed the emotions of my heart with rejoicing because of the internal woman you are. Your heart accepts so easily the things I struggle with the most.

No one should have had to do the things you had to do for me. Nevertheless, you did them faithfully, compassionately, and without hesitation. You have helped me to better understand what a Proverbs 31 woman means. You are truly an example of that spiritual model. Your love lights my way, JoAnn, and I thank God every day for sending you to me.

TABLE OF CONTENTS

First wk

second wk

ix

Foreword To 'The Ladder of Trust'
Rabbi, Dr. Charles Ian Kluge

Several years ago, I met Ron and recognized his ardent desire and passion to learn and teach the true roots of our faith in Yeshua (Jesus). His study and mastery of the Scriptures is apparent. He believes in the Scripture, "Iron sharpens iron," (Proverbs 27:17) and is always willing to test his doctrinal statements and examine them as to whether or not they line up with the Word of God.

'The Ladder of Trust' is a book for all people. It is for anyone who desires to understand the true context in which the Scriptures were written. There is contained in this book much information, research, wisdom, and knowledge. It is a must read and wealth of knowledge for any student of the Bible.

From a spiritual point of view, 'The Ladder of Trust' can only increase your faith. It expounds upon the meaning of the faith that is in your heart and spirit. The Messiah Yeshua (Jesus) is "lifted up" and revealed as the only One who could be the "Ladder."

At this time of history when we pray for and expect a major revival and return of God's people to Him, this book can help cast out divisions amongst the brethren and bring the Body of Messiah together as one. Rabbi Shaul (Paul) had urged us to study the Scriptures because they are "profitable for teaching, for reproof, for correction and for training in righteousness." (2 Timothy 3:16)

Let's begin to study and increase our faith as 'The Ladder of Trust' opens to us a deeper level of understanding God's Word through His *Ruach HaKodesh* (Holy Spirit).

Rabbi, Dr. Charles Ian Kluge
President, Gesher International, Inc.
Senior Rabbi, Congregation Gesher Shalom
Senior Rabbi, Melech Yisrael Messianic Synagogue
www.7kplusfromhome.com

Testimonials

―◦◦◦―

❝ I have only one thing to say – WOW! It is so refreshing to see a Messianic spiritual leader focus on faith as the way to accomplish the journey to salvation, and not works. You have brilliantly explained and emphasized the importance of *'beholding the ladder.'* There is so much depth that you went into.. your chapter, *'The Ladder of Trust and Your Choice'* had me actively, mentally, spiritually participating in the dialogue with fierce meditation. I was moving with every word. Praise God!❞

Ron Johnson, Pastor, Mount Zion Commandment Keeping Church of the First Born of Central Florida

"Ron Warren's *The Ladder of Trust* warms the heart and inspires the mind in a journey for your soul. This Scripture based investigation and celebration of what our Lord teaches us about faith is focused on our development of trust. Ron provides a broad variety of steps, status, and progress presented through a detailed teaching through God's Word.

Multiple perspectives in chapters and sub-points abound, such as *'Four Types of Gentiles'* presented in terms of their relationship with our Lord, knowing *'Yeshua as the Ladder'*, and *'Faith's Ladder of Trust.'* These and many others direct us upward in response to '*the call of God in your life*' as Ron writes and shares in this offering to the God of Abraham, Isaac, and Jacob."

Peter Ragan, PhD., Professor of Humanities, Embry-Riddle Aeronautical University

"This book will be both encouraging and challenging to all who read it. Encouraging to those who may be losing their trust in the Holy One, blessed be He; and challenging to those who may have a misconception of what 'faith' and 'trust' really mean, according to the true context of Scripture.

This is a book to analyze and reflect upon, not just to glance at. Sometimes, you have to go back to certain chapters and reread them to be able to internalize the content. It brings you to the point where we have to make an introspection of ourselves and judge where we are in the Ladder of Trust."

Rafael L. Ufret-Rios, Cost Control Clerk, The Peabody Hotel of Orlando

"Thank you, Ron, for writing '*The Ladder of Trust*.' Through the years, I have read a lot of books on faith and trust, but this book is the best. It is a powerful condensed book, which walks you through a lot of history and gives you a lot of knowledge. You will grow in your understanding and spiritual life by reading and applying this book. This book, '*The Ladder of Trust*', has been a blessing to me. Out of all the books this year, this is the book to buy. Again, Ron, thank you."

Constance Jones, Audioprosthologist, America's Choice Hearing Center

Acknowledgments

—◦◦◦—

To Francisco Dardiz, a special word of thanks for your belief in the worth of this project and for your support during its development and completion. This book would never have come into being without the faith you gave me. Your belief in my calling showed in your time and money. You have become a devoted friend and confidant. Your passion for this project is felt on every page. Thank you, Frank, you are deeply appreciated.

To Fred Stanley, what can I say? You have been a true brother and example. God knows your sacrifices and kindnesses. Your support for both this project and me has been strong and unwavering.

To Peter Ragan, thank you for your help. You gave me the discipline and courage to do this project. Your goal-setting abilities were needed at an extremely critical time for me. Thank you for your insights, friendship and assistance, which have been invaluable to me in the preparation of this book.

To Randy Sanford, who gave me the training and provided the platform for me to operate within my calling. You are truly a good friend. Without you, this book would never have gone beyond the 'idea' stage. Thank you very much.

To Kristen Meredith, whose unquenchable zeal and love for the Word of God along with her insatiable desire to learn has caused me to rededicate myself to the task of completing this book. Thank you, Kristen, for inspiring me to complete this project.

I would also like to thank Tony Morgan who, through his artistic talent, fashioned the illustration revealed on the cover of this book. In three hours, I saw you produce a masterpiece. Again, thank you, Tony.

To Rabbi Charles Kluge, my mentor, my teacher, my spiritual leader, and one of my best friends. You have given me moral and spiritual support in the production of this book, and agreed to do the foreword. You have taught me more about vision, mission, and focus then any other person. Thank you very much.

A special thanks needs to be given to Hilda Porter, whose advice helped to make this book happen.

A very special thanks deserves to be given to my son, Robert. His help and invaluable advice on sentence structure is greatly appreciated. Your sense of focus inspired me in the structure of this book. Your help in the editing deserves special thanks. Your help on the back copy of this book shows your talent. Without you, Robert, I do not think that this book would have been completed. Thanks again.

To Ira Michaelson, whose influence forced me to rethink some of the concepts that I believed. You were instrumental in my focusing of this book. My understanding of faith and trust deepened based on your teachings and our debates.

To Jeff Leibowitz, thanks for your encouragement and constructive criticism regarding the construction of the book.

To David Taylor, who taught me never to give a yes-or-no answer without first laying its foundation. David, you have no idea how many times I would have been misunderstood if this process had not been applied. Thanks again.

To Iona Burgdorf, my sister, who became a living example of the person with the heart of Ruth. In a very trying two-week period, you demonstrated the caring with our mother that Ruth did with Naomi. Your example inspired me to continue writing this book.

Last, but not the least, to you, the reader. You have shown your trust in me as a Messianic bible teacher by purchasing this book. I pray I never violate your trust. Thank you for giving me your trust and faith.

Preface

"*Faith is embedded in Trust.*" These five words continue to repeat itself in my mind. Sometimes it sounds like a skipping CD. These five words destroy faith as a force, which is taught by a number of leaders. I found that as my trust in God increased, my faith grew.

In my studies, I realized that as my level of faith grew, it was moving me through the uses of the seven pieces of furniture of the tabernacle. This connection became the basis for this book.

My spiritual journey took me from being a skeptical, analytical agonistic to being a born-again, Bible-loving Messianic believer. I enjoy the studies of Messianic apologetics and the histories of Judaism and Christianity. By using apologetics and the histories, I attempt to defend the authority and authenticity of the scriptures when asked.

I realized there needed to be qualifications on exactly what is meant when using certain terminology. I also realized that the histories created a conflict between the Torah (the five books of Moses), and the renewed covenant that Yeshua (Jesus) taught.

These histories produced two very different religions from scriptures – one Jewish, the other Christian. It is a fact that history does not establish what is true or false. It does show what people, centuries after the fact, have chosen and is a record of how these choices have been acted out. True Messianic Judaism is the *"bridge"* that can connect these two interpretations of histories into *"one new man."*

I pray that the conclusion you reach in reading this book is that this scripture will become your mission statement as a believer in the Jewish Messiah:

"My message and my preaching were not in persuasive words of wisdom, but in demonstration of the Spirit and of power, that your faith might not rest on the wisdom of man, but on the power of God" (1 Corinthians 2:4-5 ASV)

DEFINING TERMS

To read this book with clarity, certain terms must first be understood. If they are not, you may find this book to be very confusing. The following terms are important to know:

Afikomen – the piece of matzo hidden at the start of the Passover Seder, and is eaten at the end of the festive meal. It is the only Greek item on a Hebrew table. It means, "that which comes after."

Balsam – is the oil from the flower of the balsam plant. According to the Talmud, it was one of the ingredients used to make the incense for the tabernacle.

Bavli - the Mishnah and the Babylonian Gemara (commentaries) also known as the Babylonian Talmud.

B.C.E – stands for "Before the Common Era" (or B.C.).

Bet Din – (literally: *"House of Judgment"*) is a Jewish religious ruling council. The last one recorded in Scripture is found in Acts 15.

Brit Hadashah – is the renewed covenant (See Appendix 4), which is also known as the New Testament.

Cassia – is a spice, a type of cinnamon, taken from the buds of the cassia plant. According to the Talmud, it was one of the ingredients used to make the incense for the tabernacle.

CE – stands for "Common Era" (or A.D., Anno Domini: *"In the year of our Lord"*).

Cinnamon – is a spice taken by drying the bark of the tropical Ceylon cinnamon tree or shrub. According to the Talmud, it was one of the ingredients used to make the incense for the tabernacle.

Clove – is the bud of the flower taken from the myrtle tree. According to the Talmud, it was one of the ingredients used to make the incense for the tabernacle.

Cohen Gadol – is Hebrew for the high priest

Costus – is a type of ginger. According to the Talmud, it was one of the ingredients used to make the incense for the tabernacle.

Frankincense – is an aromatic resin taken from the boswellia tree, a tree in Arabia. It was used in incense and perfumes. It was also known as the "Oil of Lebanon." It is mentioned in Exodus 30:34 as one of the ingredients in the making of the incense for the tabernacle.

Galbanum – an aromatic gum resin from certain Persian species. It is mentioned in Exodus 30:34 as a sweet spice to be used in the making of the incense for the tabernacle. Rashi, a famous Jewish rabbi, comments on this passage that galbanum is bitter, and was included in the incense as a reminder of deliberate and unrepentant sinners.

Gemara – is a collection of commentaries on the Mishnah. They were originally written in Aramaic, codified around 550 C.E., and consist of 63 tractates.

Go'el – is Hebrew for "kinsman redeemer."

Goyim - the generic Hebrew word for Gentiles.

HaSatan – means the devil, Satan.

Keritot – (literally: *"Excisions"*) is a tractate in the Talmud, which deals with the commandments as well as the sacrifices, associated with their transgressions.

Kosher – refers to the Jewish dietary laws as recorded in the Jewish book, *"The Laws of Kashrus"* by Rabbi Binyomin Forst.

Biblical Kosher – refers to the Jewish dietary instructions as recorded in Leviticus 11.

Messiah – is the Anointed One (Christ).

Midrashim – are the ancient rabbinical commentaries on the Hebrew Bible (Tanakh). The word, "midrash" occurs twice in the Hebrew Bible: 2 Chronicles 13:22 and 24:27.

Mikvah – is a specific type of bath designed for the purpose of ritual washing in Judaism.

Mishkan – is Hebrew for the tabernacle.

Mishnah – is the Oral Law in condensed written form, codified in 200 C.E.

Myrrh – is the resin from the sap of the myrrh tree. Its perfumes and incense was worth more that its weight in gold. Also known as *"Stacte,"* it is mentioned in Exodus 30:34 as one of the ingredients used in the making of the incense for the tabernacle.

Parsha – refers to a section of a Bible book in the Tanakh (Hebrew Bible). These divisions are found in modern day Torah scrolls of all Jewish communities (Ashkenazic, Sephardic, and Yemenite)

Phylactery – refers to the Greek term for Judaic leather boxes worn on the arm and head, which contain scrolls inscribed with specific biblical verses. The verses are Exodus 13:1-16, and Deuteronomy 6:4-9 and 11:13-21.

Rosh Hashanah – (literally: "Head of the Year") refers to the Jewish New Year, also known as "The Day of the Blowing of the Shofar" (Leviticus 23:24), "The Day of Judgment", and "The Day of Remembrance."

Ruach Hakodesh – is the Holy Spirit and Breath of God

Saffron – is a spice that comes from the purple flower of the *"saffron crocus"* plant. It contains more than 150 aroma-yielding compounds. According to the Talmud, it was one of the ingredients used to make the incense for the tabernacle.

Sanhedrin – is an assembly of judges, its spiritual basis coming from Numbers 11:16. There were two classes of rabbinical courts called Sanhedrin. The '*Great Sanhedrin*' had 71 judges who were the supreme authority and legislative body in ancient Israel. A lower Sanhedrin in each city consisted of 23 judges.

Septuagint – is a name given to the Koine Greek version of the Tanakh (Hebrew Bible) translated in stages between the third and first century B.C.E. in Alexandria.

Shavuot – (literally: "The Festival of Weeks") is the Jewish wheat harvest holiday. It is also known as the "Festival of Reaping", "The Day of the First Fruits", and "The Day of Remembrance."

Shchinah – means the physical presence of God.

Shema – refers to the Jewish declaration of faith as recorded in Deuteronomy 6:4.

Simchat Torah – is a Hebrew term, which means "rejoicing with/of the Torah." It means the annual cycle of reading the Torah is completed and began anew. It is one of the happiest days in the Jewish calendar.

Spikenard – is oil taken from the Spikenard flowering plant and used for perfume and incense. It is also known as 'nard,' and is mentioned twice in the Song of Solomon (1:12 and 4:13). It is also mentioned in Mark 14:3 and John 12:3, when Mary, the sister of Lazarus, uses nard ointment to anoint the head and feet of Yeshua. This ointment was very expensive (John 12:5), and was used when a unnamed woman anointed the Messiah in Luke 7:37-50.

Sukkot – (literally: "*Booths*") is the festival known as the "Feast of Booths", the "Feast of Tabernacles", or the "Feast of Ingathering."

Targums – refers to the Aramaic translations of the Tanakh (Old Testament). There are three known Jewish Targums:

"*Targum Onkelos*" on the Torah, the "*Jerusalem Targum*", and "*Targum Pseudo Jonathan*", covering the Prophets, with the exception of Ezra, Nehemiah, and Daniel.

T'shuvah – means to repent; to turn around.

Talmud – is the Mishnah and its commentaries (Gemara). There are two Talmuds: The *Jerusalem Talmud* and the *Babylonian Talmud*. The Mishnah and the Gemara are considered part of the Torah of Moses by Orthodox Jews.

Tanakh – is the Hebrew Bible, also known in Christianity as the "*Old Testament*" (see Appendix 4).

Tefillin – is also known as 'Phylacteries.' They are two boxes containing biblical verses used in traditional Jewish prayers by Jewish men above the age of thirteen. It comes from the interpretations found in Exodus 13:9, 16, and Deuteronomy 6:8, 11:18.

Torah – for a Messianic believer and about 70 percent of the Jewish people, it refers to the five books of Moses (Genesis, Exodus, Leviticus, Numbers, and Deuteronomy).

Tosefta – is a more complete written form of the oral law.

Tractate – is an essay. In the Jewish faith, it is on the Talmud. Christianity also has tractates.

T'zilah – is the Hebrew term for water baptism.

Tzitzis – are the fringes or tassels worn by observant Jews on the corners of four-cornered garments, obeying the Torah instructions of Numbers 15:38 and Deuteronomy 22:12.

Vulgate – is an early fifth century version of the Bible in Latin, with the 'Old Testament' translated directly from the Hebrew Tanakh instead of the Greek Septuagint.

Yeshua – is the Hebrew name for Jesus.

Yoma – is a treatise in the Mishnah covering the service performed on the Jewish Day of Atonement. It is divided into eight chapters.

Yom Kippur – is the Jewish Day of Repentance, also known as the Day of Atonement.

I. WHAT THIS BOOK CAN DO FOR YOU

*"The truth which makes man free is for the most part the truth
which men prefer not to hear."*

Herbert Agar (1897-1980)

I. WHAT THIS BOOK CAN DO FOR YOU

—⚬⚬⚬—

> *"Whom shall (God) teach knowledge? And whom shall He make to understand doctrine? Them that are weaned (taken off) from the milk, and drawn (removed) from the breasts. For precept must be upon precept, precept upon precept; line upon line, line upon line; here a little, and there a little..."* (Isaiah 28:9-10 KJV)

FAITH IS EMBEDDED IN TRUST

Has your faith ever been tested? How did you deal with it? Would you like to have your trust in God strengthened? How would you increase your faith? What process would you use? If you were given a way that could help you increase your faith in God, would you use it?

As the cheshire cat pointed out to Alice in Lewis Carroll's book, *"Alice in Wonderland:"* *"If you don't know where you are going, any road will get you there."*[1] This book can be called, "a road map with directions." The process in this book will not only give you a path to walk, but can also increase your knowledge and open the door to abilities you never knew you had. Often God will remove the familiar things in your life to establish a new foundation in your life.

For many people, the distinction between the two words, faith and trust, is unclear. The lack of this understanding results in a great deal of overlap in many ways. The missions of this book are to emphasize the importance of understanding these differences and help you grow in the knowledge and the love of God through its process.

"Faith is embedded in trust." These five words – faith is embedded in trust – declare the Hebraic understanding of faith. Trust is essential to faith. Why? When faith ceases to exist, trust disappears. When faith increases, trust grows. You can have faith without trust, but you cannot have trust without faith. Faith is not belief without proof. It is part of trust without reservation.

Trust can produce seven levels of faith. They are: common, little, temporary, strong, creative (also known as great), active, and divine faith. As your faith grows through hearing the Word of God, you become empowered to climb the ladder of trust towards the object of that trust – in this case, God. This is the meaning behind the illustration on the front cover of this book.

Go to any bookstore. You will find a large number of religious books on the topic of faith. Why, then, do we need another? I believe the levels of trust and faith can be introduced and explained in a concise manner. The differences confuse many sincere students who want a richer, deeper understanding of their walk with God.

The word *"faith"* is often misused, both at the pulpit and in the popular religious media.

On most Sunday mornings, for instance, you are likely to hear quite a few evangelists talking about faith on television.

They speak of faith as if it were an object, a thing, or a force. However, they do not really explain what faith is, where it comes from, or how it is to be used.

Because the word 'faith' has been so overused, it has lost much of its historical meaning. If you understand the context in scripture when the word 'faith' is used, it is meant to convey tremendous meaning, and it is loaded with power. True faith, the ladder of understanding, represents the path to clarity, both the goal and the hope of this book.

The Greek translation of Hebrews 11:1 literally says, *"Now faith is the reality of things being hoped for, the proof of things not being seen."* The first definition in *Webster's Third New International Dictionary* defines faith as: "the act or state of wholeheartedly and steadfastly believing in the existence, power, and benevolence of a supreme being, of having confidence in his providential care, and of being loyal to his will as revealed or believed in."

Because the dictionary lists the oldest and most primary of a word's definitions first, the rest of the definitions demonstrate how the meaning of the English word 'faith' has changed over the centuries. The second definition, for example, is a: "firm or unquestioning belief in something for which there is no proof."

The third definition is "an assurance, promise, or pledge of fidelity, loyalty, or performance." The fourth definition is "authority, credit, or credibility." The fifth definition is "something that is believed or adhered to especially with strong conviction." Finally, the sixth definition is "the faith spoken of as the true religion from the point of view of the speaker."

These definitions show a steady weakening and secularization of the English word 'faith' over time.

It is from this sixth definition that statements such as the following arise: "He was not healed because of his lack of faith" Or "If you only believe, _____(fill in the blank)."

In 1904, when the stage production of *"Peter Pan"* began playing in London, the flying hero of Never Never Land fascinated children.

Some were so thrilled, in fact, that they wanted to be just like Peter, who said, "If you only believe, you can fly!" When distraught parents began contacting J. M. Barrie, the writer of the Peter Pan stories, about children who had injured themselves while attempting to fly, he changed the script so that Tinker Bell's fairy dust was needed—in addition to belief—in order to fly.

How does trust connect to faith? Imagine standing at the foundation of two staircases. One staircase heads up, the other, down. What determines your choice? In this context, it is not your circumstances. Your heart determines your choice. The choice you take will affect both your emotions and your character.

If you take the staircase upward, you start with trust. As your trust increases, you develop faith. Trust and faith help you develop initiative. When you apply your initiative, while increasing your faith and trust, you develop self-esteem. When you apply your self-esteem, initiative, faith and trust, you develop self-confidence.

When these characteristics become a part of your character, you develop intimacy, which involves communication. As your intimacy and communication increases, so does your creativity, which involves reaching your optimum productivity. You finally reach the top step: integrity. However, this process starts with trust.

Trust requires faith. Faith is related to risk, and risk is related to fear.

If you take the staircase downward, you start with mistrust. Mistrust will lead you into shame and/or doubt.

As your mistrust, shame, and doubt increases, so will your guilt, which will move you into a strong inferiority complex. As these characteristics become a part of your character, you develop role confusion, which produces isolation.

The more you move away from creativity, the closer you get to stagnation and finally despair.

To get back to trust, you first have to go back up the downward staircase, backtracking despair, stagnation, isolation, role confusion, inferiority, guilt, shame, and doubt, then mistrust. This is why, when trust is destroyed, it is hard to get it back.

To get to the top step of the upward staircase of trust – integrity - you need to do two steps. First: plot a wise course that maximizes each step along the way. Then, avoid the deteriorating effects that accumulate on the downward staircase. This book is designed to help you in this process.

TWO END RESULT FOUNDATIONAL CONCEPTS

If you loaded a Boeing 747 airplane with theologians, flew around the world seven times, and all the while the theologians discussed the Holy Scriptures, when the airplane landed, they would not all agree.

This is a religious reference book. If you are a believer, this book is teaching to the choir. If you are an agnostic, this book is designed, by applying reason and logic, to make you reconsider your position without preaching. If you are Jewish, this book is to introduce you to your Jewish Messiah through the tabernacle. If you are a Christian, this book will share with you the strength of the Jewish roots of your faith. If you are just starting your life, this book will strengthen your will to do, not just believe.

If you are at the end of your life and dying, you are hungry for faith. This book was written to help you to grow in your faith, and through that process, your trust in God.

This book has a great deal of information, producing knowledge. Knowledge not applied is a student loan. When knowledge is added with experience, it produces wisdom. Information alone is not power. You can give a child the blueprints to build a computer, but the data would be completely useless to him.

Knowledge is power, but unless applied, would also be useless. The child could understand the blueprints, but if he did not have the parts to assemble the computer, it would still be useless.

Knowledge applied wins. Knowledge when applied becomes powerful. That process is called wisdom. It is through wisdom that practical, positive changes, even miracles, can occur.

You can receive a miracle in the material world but it must be preceded by a change in your own character. Physical reality of your miracle and the human nature of your character are intimately connected. You become placed into the position for your miracle by applying faith and the life applications connected to the ladder of trust and the tabernacle.

This book is designed to answer these questions, among others:

- What is the meaning of the word "Memra," and why is it important?
- How do you climb the ladder of trust?
- What is the 'bill of charges' against us?
- Do you have the faith of Barabbas?
- What is the difference between the Son of God and the Son of Man?
- Does 'blind faith' exist?
- Who has more blind faith, a believer or an atheist?
- What was Pascal's wager?
- What are the four battlefields of faith?
- How does the ladder of trust connect to the tabernacle?
- Where are you on the ladder of trust?

People have a starting point that determines their belief. My starting points for understanding the Word of God are two basic foundational concepts:

1) Yeshua (Jesus) was and is Jewish.
2) The Scriptures are Jewish.

If you can accept these two basic foundational concepts, this book will open your understanding and renew your mind. The scriptures quoted are from the King James Version (KJV), the American Standard Version (ASV), The New International Version (NIV), The Amplified Version, (AMP), and the Complete Jewish Bible (CJB).

James 3:1 writes about the awesome responsibility and the most important danger of being a bible teacher: *"Be not many (of you) teachers, my brethren, knowing that we shall receive heavier judgment"* (ASV).

Two Scriptures were used for guidance on writing this book because of a holy fear of God and the 'heavier judgment'. The first Scripture reads: *"But sanctify the Lord God in your hearts: and be ready always to **give an answer** [emphasis mine] to every man that asketh you **a reason of the hope** [emphasis mine] that is in you with meekness and fear"* (I Peter 3:15 KJV).

The second scripture reads: *"Do all you can to present yourself to God, as someone worthy of His approval, as a worker with no need to be ashamed, because he deals straight-forwardly with the Word of the Truth"* (2 Timothy 2:15 CJB).

TWO WAYS TO INTERPRET SCRIPTURES

Allow me to share some basic groundwork before continuing. Do you consider the Scriptures as truth? If yes, how do you?

Do you see the Scriptures as *relative truth* or a*bsolute truth*? Relative truth means you determine the truth of the Scriptures based on your experiences and feelings, which are changeable. Absolute truth means you establish the truth of the Scriptures as not changing, but alive.

Why is this important? Your answer will determine how you handle the Word of God. It also determines how you look at God. The difference is between a "hip-pocket" God, where God has been turned into your personal genie, and a God who is sovereign. If you chose a God who is supreme, you see the Scriptures as absolute truth, even if you do not like to hear it.

There are two basic ways to interpret Scripture. The first way is to draw meaning from the text itself. The second way is to read a meaning into the text, which is foreign to the literal sense. By interpreting from the text itself, no verse can be interpreted that would conflict with what is clearly taught elsewhere in Scripture.

Interpreting the Scriptures from the text does not line up with our politically correct world, but it is the truth if you accept the Scriptures as the Word of God.

Some religious leaders believe that "*rightly dividing the Word of truth*" (2 Timothy 2:15), means destroying the context of the Scriptures, ignoring Scriptures that will destroy their doctrines, or misinterpreting the Scriptures to support their doctrine. This book is designed to draw meaning from the text itself.

Any Scripture taken out of its context is a "pretext". To read a foreign meaning into the text, otherwise known as "proof texting," would be using the Scriptures for your conclusion, not God's.

A lawyer was in the hospital dying of cancer. His best friend, a believer, came to visit him, and found the lawyer going frantically through the Scriptures.

"Jim, What are you doing?" the friend asked.

The lawyer replied, "I am looking for a loophole."

A loophole example of a pretext Scripture is the following:

You want God working in your life so, through prayer, you decided to open the Scriptures at random, pick a verse, and use it for guidance that day. I call this process "Bible roulette."

Following this goal, you open your Bible, pick a verse, and read "*And Judas went out and hanged himself*" (Matthew 27:5). You shoot a Gideon prayer to God, asking for the prayer of the second chance. Finished, you again open your Bible, pick a verse, and read "*Go thou, and do likewise*" (Luke 10:37).

Any Scripture used out of context is not the Word of God. It places you in error and spiritually dead. Judge this work of love within the context of the Word of God.

You are, after reading this book and according to John 3:21, required to walk in the light God has given you. It reads in the King James Bible, "*But he that **doeth** truth **cometh** [emphasis mine] to the light, that his deeds may be made manifest, that they are wrought in God*" (KJV).

What happens if you do not walk in that light? Hosea 4:6 will give you the answer.

"*My people are destroyed for lack of knowledge: because thou hast rejected knowledge, I will also reject thee, that thou shalt be no priest to me: seeing thou hast forgotten the law of thy God, I also will forget thy children*" (KJV).

God has also placed a warning concerning this light of the Word given to you. Luke 11:35 states: "*Take heed therefore that the light which is in thee be not darkness.*" Romans 1:18-32 tells you what happens when the light God gives you becomes darkness. Read it, than settle your mind on what to do with the light given to you.

II. YESHUA – JACOB'S LADDER

"He who takes truth for his guide, and duty for his end,
may safety trust to God's Providence to lead him aright."

Blaise Pascal (1623-1662)

II. YESHUA – JACOB'S LADDER

―⁓⁓―

> **"The mind of man plans his way, but the Lord directs his steps" (Proverbs 16 :9 ASV)**

YESHUA AS THE LADDER

What do Scriptures say about Yeshua as your ladder?

"Yeshua saw Nathaniel coming to him, and saith of him, Behold an Israelite indeed, in whom is no guile! Nathaniel saith unto him, Whence knowest thou me? Yeshua answered and said unto him, Before that Phillip called thee, when thou wast under the fig tree, I saw thee."

"Nathaniel answered and saith unto him, Rabbi, thou art the Son of God; thou art the King of Israel. Yeshua answered and said unto him, Because I said unto thee, I saw thee under the fig tree, believest thou? thou shalt see greater things than these."

"And he saith unto him, Verily, verily, I say unto you, Hereafter ye shall see heaven open, and the angels of God ascending and descending upon the Son of man" (John1:47-51 KJV).

The four lists of disciples in Scripture - Matthew 10:2-4, Mark 3:16-19, Luke 6:12-16, Acts 1:13 – testify that Bartholomew is a disciple, yet Nathaniel, who in these verses was called, is not listed. Bartholomew is a family name. The *Hebrew-Greek Study Bible, New American Standard Version*, in its footnotes on Matthew 10:3, lists Bartholomew as the son of Taimai. Taimai is the Hebrew translation for the Greek word Ptolemy. The Hebrew idiom *"each man sitting under his own vine and fig tree"* refers to well being, and prosperity. Yeshua's reference of Nathaniel *"under the fig tree"* may indicate that he was wealthy.

We know that quite often, for whatever reason, the rabbis of the Second Temple period taught under fig trees and that students spent time sitting under fig trees meditating and studying the Torah. It is on one such occasion that Yeshua saw Nathaniel sitting under a fig tree studying.[2]

Moreover, judging from the nature of the dialogue between them, it seems evident that Nathaniel was mediating on the weekly parsha for this time of the year, parashat Vayeitzei! [3]

There are three spiritual truths seen in this story. The first spiritual truth shows that the ladder was upon the earth, but the top reached into heaven. Yeshua stood on the earth in empty human form, but He never left the bosom of His Father.

"No man hath seen God at any time; the only begotten Son, which is in the bosom of the Father, he hath declared him" (John 1:18 KJV).

"And no man hath ascended up to heaven, but he that came down from heaven, even the Son of man, which is in heaven" (John 3:13 KJV).

The second spiritual truth in this story concerns Jacob seeing the angels of God going up and down the ladder. The implication is clear that Yeshua is claiming to be the ladder upon which one can gain access to God! Just as the ladder in Jacob's dream was the vehicle by which the heavenly hosts had access to the throne of God, so it is that through Yeshua the Messiah that sinful humanity may have access to the Holy One. Later in His ministry, Yeshua made the same claim in John 14:6, *"I am the way, the truth, and the life: no man comes to the Father, but through me"* (ASV).[4]

You have access to God through Yeshua, your ladder. Without this ladder, there can be no access. If Yeshua is your Ladder, you are able to ascend to God in heaven by Him alone. Through the Jewish Messiah, God comes down to you and gives the power, by His grace, to ascend.

The third spiritual truth is outstanding. Grace always flows downhill, never uphill. God is above the ladder. He made all the promises of grace to Jacob in the Torah. The baton has been passed again, and it was the changing of the guard for the Abrahamic covenant from Jacob to Yeshua.

Again, if Yeshua is your ladder, you are under a covenant, and all the promises of God's grace comes down to you through Yeshua, your mediator and your ladder. Romans 5:10-11 says:

"For if we were reconciled with God through his Son's death when we were enemies, how much more will we be delivered by his life, now that we are reconciled! And not only will we be delivered in the future, but we are boasting about God right now, because he has acted through our Lord Yeshua the Messiah, through whom we have already received that reconciliation" (CJB).

You are not under a covenant and cannot claim God's promises if Yeshua is not your ladder.

THE "TETRAGRAMMATON"

The word *"Lord"* in many verses of the Tanakh is the *"Tetragrammaton,"* the four-letter word for God, YHVH. YHVH means *"The Self-Existent One."* It is applied in Scripture as *"The God of the Covenant."* This is God's most common name, occurring six thousand, eight hundred twenty-three times in Scripture. It also means "The Eternal," which has no regard for time or space.

When the Greek language became the standard, the tetragrammation YHVH lost its impact. The Septuagint, which is the Greek translation of the Tanakh, substituted YHVH, with the Greek word, '*kurios*' for the word, '*Lord*.' This confused the Jewish reader because Hebrew already had another word for "*Lord*"(*Adown*). The Vulgate, which is the Latin translation of the Bible, uses the word, '*dominus*.'

"And God said unto Moses, I AM THAT I AM [emphasis mine]: and he said, Thus shalt thou say unto the children of Israel, I AM [emphasis mine] hath sent me unto you" (Exodus 3:14 KJV).

The English translation of this verse is '*I AM WHO I AM*' or '*I WILL BE WHO I WILL BE*,' but the literal Hebrew word translation for YHVH is "*I AM, I AM*". The first "*I AM*" is masculine, and the last "*I AM*" is feminine: the nature of God.

Let's look at another verse: *"Thou hast ascended on high. You have led captivity captive: Thou hast received gifts for men; yea, for the rebellious also, that the LORD God might dwell among them"* (Psalm 68:18 KJV).

Again, the word "LORD" in this verse is the Hebrew word YHVH. It gives a sense of God becoming a salvation to His creatures.

This name was only mentioned one time during the year at the time of Yeshua. That day was Yom Kippur, known as the Jewish Day of Atonement. If this name was said any other time, it was considered blasphemy, which meant death by stoning.

Orthodox Jews today would use the word "*Hashem*," meaning "*The Name*," when they came to this name while reading Scriptures. A scribe creating a new Torah scroll would, every time he came to this place to write "*The Name*," go through a mikvah and change clothes before continuing, and pray. Leviticus 24:16 reads:

"And he that blasphemes the name of the LORD [YHVH], he shall surely be put to death, and all the congregation shall certainly stone him: as will the stranger, as he that is born in the land, when he blasphemeth the name of the Lord [YHVH], shall be put to death" (KJV).

The same scribe, because of this verse among others, when having to retire a Torah scroll, would bury it, not burn it. To do anything different would be to destroy the name of God. It also explains the reason why they write the name as "G-d."

Jehovah – The Problem

The attack of certain doctrines is not the purpose of this book, but the understanding of doctrine through a Hebraic understanding is. With this goal in mind, let's continue. When a Jewish person reading from the Torah scroll in the synagogue came to this name, YHVH, he would replace it by saying, "Adonai" meaning "Lord," another name for God. When the vowels were added to the Torah writings between 890 – 940 C.E. by a group of Jewish scholars, the vowels for "Adonai" were added under the name YHVH.

This was to remind the people to say "Adonai" rather than taking His name in vain. The text became known as the "Masoretic text."

During the middle ages, the first English translators, who were not familiar with this Jewish understanding, assumed the consonants of YHVH with the vowels for "Adonai" formed the name of God. They had no reason to believe that the vowels of YHVH were incorrect.

When they transcribed this name, they wrote it the way it sounded and created a non-Jewish, non-Hebrew name for God: "Iehovah." The first time it occurred was in Tyndale's translation in 1530.

The letter J did not come into existence until late in the 1500s and did not become popular until the 1600s. Any name beginning with the letter J, including the name of Jesus, is only about four hundred years old.

The exchange of the "I" to the "J" in "Jehovah" is a result of Martin Luther's transcribing of the Biblical Hebrew name, YHVH, in his German translation of the Masoretic text, first published in 1534. This is how the name "Jehovah" came into being. There is no "J" in Hebrew and no biblical word, in Hebrew or Greek, called "Jehovah." Moses would not have given this name to a created being.

The religion that most commonly uses the name "Jehovah" is the Jehovah's Witnesses. They believe that God's personal name should not be overshadowed by the above titles, and they oftentimes refer to Psalm 83:18 as a common place in most translations to find the name Jehovah still used in place of "LORD".

It reads, *"That men may know that thou, whose name alone is JEHOVAH [emphasis mine], art the most high over all the earth"* (Psalm 83:18 KJV).

Today, out of the many times the name YHVH appears in Scripture, it is only translated 4 times as "JEHOVAH" in the King James Bible: Exodus 6:3; Psalm 83:18; Isaiah 12:2; and Isaiah 26:4

Yahweh (YHWH) – The Problem

There is also no "W" in Hebrew and no biblical word, in Hebrew or Greek, called "Yahweh."

The religion that commonly uses the name "Yahwah" is the Sacred Name Movement, which teaches that unless you use the Hebrew name and only the Hebrew name for God, you will be eternally damned. They use, among others, the 1966 Jerusalem Bible translation.

If you allow for variant spellings, than you can go back to 1881 for the first time "Yahweh" was used in Scripture. It can be found when J. M. Rodwell's "Isaiah" used the form "Jahveh."

In 1863, William Smith, in his book "*A Dictionary of the Bible*" used "Yahweh" for YHVH but added " *even if these writers were entitled to speak with authority, their evidence only tends to show in how many different ways the four letters of the word 'YHVH' could be pronounced in Greek characters, and throws no light either upon its real pronunciation or its punctuation.*"[5]

How do you pronounce "Jehovah" in Portuguese? It is "Yahweh."

Yeshua – The "I AM"

During the time of Yeshua, the religious leaders would never have accepted a created being having this name. Yeshua upset His generation when He said, "*Before Abraham was, I AM [emphasis mine]*" (John 8:58 KJV). The religious leaders understood what Yeshua meant. The next verse (John 8:59 KJV) says they "*took up stones to throw at him.*"

Yeshua continued to push the envelope, and used this term eight additional times in the Gospel of John to restate His deity:

"**I AM** *[emphasis mine]* the Light of the World" (John 8:12, 9:5 KJV).

"**I AM** *[emphasis mine]* the Bread of Life" (John 6:35, 48 KJV).

"**I AM** *[emphasis mine]* the Door of the Sheep" (John 10:7 KJV).

"**I AM** *[emphasis mine]* the Good Shepherd" (John 10:11, 14 KJV).

"**I AM** *[emphasis mine]* the Resurrection and the Life" (John 11:26-27 KJV).

"**I AM** *[emphasis mine]* the Way, the Truth, and the Life" (John 14:6 KJV).

"I AM *[emphasis mine]* the True Vine"(John 15:1, 5 KJV).

"I AM *[emphasis mine] He"* (John 18:5, 8 KJV).

When God is speaking of Himself, He uses the word *Ehyeh* ("I AM"). When God is being spoken of (YHVH), He is the God of redemption fulfilling His promise. When Yeshua used the "I AM," He was showing a relationship between Himself and God.

In Jeremiah 23:5 the descendant of David is clearly identified as the King Messiah: *"Behold, the days are coming, declares the LORD; when I will raise for David **a righteous Branch** [emphasis mine]; And He will reign as king and act wisely, and shall do justice and righteousness in the land."* (NAS). In the next verse you read: *"In his days Judah will be saved and Israel will dwell safely: This is the name by which he will be called: **THE LORD YOUR RIGHTEOUSNESS** [emphasis mine]"* (Jeremiah 23:6 NIV).

The "righteous Branch," the name given to the Messiah by Jeremiah, is applied to "The Lord your Righteousness," which contains the divine name YHVH. It was a clear indication that the Messiah is to be a divine being.

Demanding pronunciation of the Messiah's name in one specific language is a non-issue. The Messiah's name, even in His own day, was pronounced different ways.

Jews in the time of Yeshua commonly spoke Aramaic. The Gospels give evidence to the fact that Yeshua also spoke in Aramaic by leaving certain of His words not translated from Aramaic (Mark 5:41; 7:34).

In Aramaic, Yeshua's name would have been pronounced "Yesu" by the Galileans (including Yeshua Himself), and as "Yeshu" in southern Israel, because they were typically able to pronounce the "sh" sound of the Hebrew letter "shin," whereas northern Israelites could not, as proven by Scriptures.

"And the Gileadites took the passages of Jordan before the Ephraimites:"

"and it was so, that when those Ephraimites which were escaped said, Let me go over; that the men of Gilead said unto him, Art thou an Ephraimite? If he said, Nay;"

"Then said they unto him, Say now Shibboleth: and he said Sibboleth: for he could not frame to pronounce it right. Then they took him, and slew him at the passages of Jordan: and there fell at that time of the Ephraimites forty and two thousand" (Judges 12:5-6 KJV).

In addition to Aramaic, however, most Jews spoke (or were at least familiar with) Hebrew, Greek and Latin. All of these languages were spoken in Judea because it was a popular trading route. When interacting with various individuals, the Messiah would have heard His name pronounced three or four different ways.

The primary language within the Roman Empire was Greek. The reason Greeks would call Yeshua "Iesous" was because it is the way the Hebrew "Yeshua," or the Aramaic "Yesu," would have sounded to the Greek.

The Greeks did not have a "y" sound in their alphabet for the Hebrew letter "yod." They would begin Yeshua's name with a long "e" sound. In addition, they did not have a letter for the "sh" sound of the Hebrew letter "shin." This would force them to make the last syllable begin with an "s" sound.

For the ending of this syllable, the Greeks simply added another "s," known as *sigma*. This was a common addition to the end of masculine names in the nominative case. "Iesous" was a direct transliteration from Hebrew to Greek.

"For then will I turn to the people a pure language, that they may all call upon the name of the LORD (YHVH), to serve him with one consent" (Zephaniah 3:9 KJV).

This verse says that other nations will pray to YHVH. There is a great difference between saying that they will pray to YHVH (referring to His person), and saying that they will pronounce His name in Hebrew.

A person is not the same as his language. It would be no different if you spoke Spanish as your native tongue, rather than English. You are still the same person. Your physical reality does not change.

To define a person in terms of his language is illogical. In order to substantiate this claim, it would have to be demonstrated how the pronunciation of someone's name, or the use of a certain language, could radically change or alter one's existence.

THE PASSING OF THE COVENANT

The Abrahamic covenant was passed by oath to Isaac, not Ishmael. The vision of the ladder also applied to the passing of the Abrahamic covenant from Isaac to Jacob, not Esau:

"And, behold, the LORD stood above it, and said, I am the LORD God of Abraham thy father, and the God of Isaac: the land whereon thou liest, to thee will I give it, and to thy seed; And thy seed shall be as the dust of the earth, and thou shalt spread abroad to the west, and to the east, and to the north, and to the south: and in thee and in thy seed shall all the families of the earth be blessed. And, behold, I am with thee, and will keep thee in all places whither thou goest, and will bring thee again into this land; for I will not leave thee, until I have done that which I have spoken to thee of" (Genesis 28:13-15 KJV).

In verse 13, God confirmed Jacob's chosen status. In verse 14, God gave Jacob his purpose and mission. In verse 15, God said He would be with Jacob and bring him back to the land of Canaan.

Jacob called the location, "Beth-el," meaning both "House of God" and the "Gate of Heaven." The vision was the changing of the guard for the Abrahamic covenant from Isaac to Jacob. The baton has been passed.

Jacob gave a conditional vow because of this vision, which is recorded in Genesis 28:20-22:

"And Jacob vowed a vow, saying, If God will be with me, and will keep me in this way that I go, and will give me bread to eat, and raiment to put on, So that I come again to my father's house in peace; then shall the LORD be my God:"

"And this stone, which I have set for a pillar, shall be God's house: and of all that thou shalt give me I will surely give the tenth unto thee" (KJV).

Based on these Scriptures, the origins of several Israelite customs were established in Jacob's descendants. First, vows became important in Israel because of the vow of Jacob. Second, the memorial at "The House of God," and is still, a holy place where God will be seen again. It became the Temple Mount in Jerusalem.

Another origin was the custom of tithing being applied in Israel. Last, but not the least, the memorial stones, different from altars, were set up to recall divine visitations so others might learn about God when they ask, "What do these stones mean?"

This is God's answer: *"to serve as a sign among you. In the future, when your children ask you, 'What do these stones mean?' tell them that the flow of the Jordan was cut off before the ark of the covenant of the Lord. When it crossed the Jordan, the waters of the Jordan you are cut off. These stones are to be a memorial to the people of Israel forever"* (Joshua 4:6-7 NIV).

WHAT IS WORSHIP?

What was Jacob's response to his vision? It was worship. What is worship? *Webster's Dictionary* has a precise meaning of worship. It lists worship as "adore, idolize, esteem worthy, reverence, homage." [6]

Yet defining biblical worship proves to be a more difficult task. Why? Biblical worship is both an attitude and an act. This forces another question: How do you walk humbly with your God? You walk in two ways: as a servant (the act), and by trust through faith (the attitude).

Through Servanthood

The believer in Yeshua is called a "Christian" only three times in Scripture (Acts 11:26; Acts 26:28; and I Peter 4:16), but in the *Brit Hadashah* the word "servant" is used a total of ninety-seven times. From that number, the body of Messiah is referred to as a "servant" forty-six times.

In Hebrew, the word servant, *"ebed,"* contains two key ingredients: action, showing the servant as a worker, and obedience.

In the *Brit Hadashah*, this term points to a relation of absolute dependence, showing the master and the servant standing on conflicting sides, the former having a full claim, the latter having a full commitment. The servant can exercise no will or initiative on his or her own.

By Trust Through Faith

"It was the same with Abraham: 'He trusted in God and was faithful to him, and that was credited to his account as righteousness.' Be assured, then, that it is those who live by trusting and being faithful who are really children of Abraham. Also the Tanakh, foreseeing that God would consider the Gentiles righteous when they live by trusting and being faithful, told the Good News to Abraham in advance by saying, "In connection with you, all the Goyim will be blessed." So then, those who rely on trusting and being faithful are blessed along with Abraham, who trusted and was faithful" (Galatians 3:6-9 CJB).

What did Abraham believe? If you can discover and believe what Abraham believed, it will also be "counted as righteousness" for you.

(1) He believed God would bring a supernatural birth, and God did.

(2) He believed God enough to offer his only son, and he did.

(3) He believed for three days his son was as good as dead, and Isaac was. *"So then, those who rely on trusting and being faithful are blessed along with Abraham, who trusted and was faithful"* (Galatians 3:9 CJB).

(4) He believed God would provide a sacrifice substitute, or raise his son from the dead, and God did.

(5) He believed on the actual mountain, God would provide Himself the substitute sacrifice, and God did.

Abraham trusted the character of the God he knew. You are asked to believe as Abraham did:

(1) You are asked to believe in a supernatural birth from a virgin.

(2) You are asked to believe God would offer His son for you.

(3) You are asked to believe His Son died and was dead for three days.

(4) You are asked to believe God raised His Son from the dead.

(5) You are asked to believe God sent His only Son to sacrifice Himself on the actual mountain region where Isaac was offered and was seen.

Will you believe it? If you do, then these Scriptures apply to you:

"So then, those who rely on trusting and being faithful are blessed along with Abraham, who trusted and was faithful" (Galatians 3:9 CJB).

In the Scriptures, there were six responses of worship by Jacob. They were: having fear before the Lord, erecting a memorial stone pillar, consecrating the stone by anointing the top with oil, naming the place "Bethel" or "House of God," making a vow and expressing his faith in God for the first time by saying, "The Lord will be my God," and promising to tithe.

"And Jacob rose up early in the morning, and took the stone that he had put for his pillows, and set it up for a pillar, and poured oil upon the top of it. And he called the name of that place Bethel: but the name of that city was called Luz at the first."

"And Jacob vowed a vow, saying, If God will be with me, and will keep me in this way that I go, and will give me bread to eat, and raiment to put on,"

"So that I come again to my father'sⁱ house in peace; then shall the LORD be my God: And this stone, which I have set for a pillar, shall be God's house: and of all that thou shalt give me I will surely give the tenth unto thee" (Genesis 28:18-22 KJV).

God, by His grace, visits His people and promises them protection (See Appendix 2) and provision so that they would be a blessing to others. You respond to Him in trust through faith, fearing Him, worshipping Him, giving offerings to Him, offering vows to Him, and making memorials for future believers according to these points.

Jacob's ladder was a hint showing that the promise would conclude in something bridging heaven and earth.

"And he dreamed, and behold a Ladder set up on the earth, and the top of it reached to heaven: and behold the angels of God ascending and descending on it. And, behold, the LORD stood above it, and said, I am the LORD God of Abraham thy father, and the God of Isaac: the land whereon thou liest, to thee will I give it, and to thy seed;"

"And thy seed shall be as the dust of the earth, and thou shalt spread abroad to the west, and to the east, and to the north, and to the south: and in thee and in thy seed shall all the families of the earth be blessed. And, behold, I am with thee, and will keep thee in all places whither thou goest, and will bring thee again into this land; for I will not leave thee, until I have done that which I have spoken to thee of" (Genesis 28:12-15 KJV).

FUNCTIONS OF A LADDER

What is the function of a ladder? A ladder is used when you need to get from a low place to a high place, or transport something from a high place to a low place.

The ladder in Jacob's vision is recorded in verse 12: *"And he dreamed, and behold a Ladder set up on the earth, and the top of it reached to heaven: and behold the angels of God ascending and descending on it"* (KJV).

This is the only time the Hebrew word *"sulam,"* meaning ladder, appears in Scripture. "The Place" quoted in this Scripture, and according to Jewish tradition, was Mt. Moriah. It is where Isaac sealed the covenant by being offered as a sacrifice. Later it became known as the Temple Mount.

Jacob was going to walk an extensive, hard road, both physical and spiritual, and he needed the encouragement of God at this point in his life.

How do you use the ladder? The ladder can be used as an analogy to define your existence. You must always work to go up. If you try to remain where you are, then gravity is going to act, pulling you down. As the ladder has many rungs and a strong foundation used to support your body, so you, if trying to improve your character, cannot advance without a solid foundation.

You need to understand three things concerning the ladder. First, everything comes in steps or stages. The ladder must be grounded firmly at the beginning stage or step. The ladder cannot stand unless it is leaning against a high place, or is a stepladder.

Second, your level of trust, which determines your way or walk, is the rungs of the ladder. As you climb higher, if the ladder is not grounded firmly, it will fall, and you will get hurt.

Third, you must learn and use its rules. Only a fool would ignore the rungs and attempt to drag himself up the left-hand pole of the ladder by his hands. How far would he get?

You need models or mentors on each of the next stages of the ladder that will be able to show and guide you upward. Do not look down, nor fear the ridicules from people below trying to stop you from going up the ladder. Instead, look up towards the top, relying upon the ladder, your mentor, and the high place on which the ladder leans.

If you encounter difficulty and slip, or come to a broken rung, all is not lost. You catch hold of the next rung and continue upward. This is normal. People are not perfect. It is like trying to lose weight overnight. You can go up or down, however, based on your goal and desire, you continue.

Sometimes you try to become perfect overnight, but that process is doomed to failure. It is a slow process, and slipping back to the old nature is a natural part of it. The trick is not to become discouraged, give up, or slide down. This is how you reach your goals.

Yeshua said He was, and is, the ladder: *"And he saith unto him, Verily, verily, I say unto you, Hereafter ye shall see heaven open, and the angels of God ascending and descending upon the Son of man"* (John 1:51 KJV).

This scriptural reference shows the 'Son of man" as the ladder. You have no other way to getting to heaven from earth, but by this ladder.

Yeshua - Your Living Ladder

Let's look at six known ways that reveal Yeshua to be your ladder. The first way shows Yeshua as your *living* ladder. The Scriptures, in Hebrews 10:20, call Yeshua "a new and living way:"

"By a new and living way, which he hath consecrated for us, through the veil, that is to say, his flesh" (Hebrews 10:20 KJV).

In this same sense, He is your new and living ladder. This ladder lives forever:

"I am he that liveth, and was dead; and, behold, I am alive forevermore, Amen; and have the keys of hell and of death" (Revelation 1:18 KJV).

The best part about this living ladder is that because He lives, all who live their lives in Him also live.

At the final judgment, you will also be able to repeat the words of Yeshua, *"I am he that liveth, and was dead, but behold I am alive forevermore, Amen"* (Revelation 1:18 KJV).

Yeshua - Your Long Ladder

The second way reveals Yeshua to be your *long* ladder, which are the two natures of your Redeemer - God and man - in one person. As man, He was set up on Earth (Galatians 4:4-5), and as God, He is always in Heaven. The union of these two natures is the mystery of all mysteries.

"And without controversy great is the mystery of Godliness: God was manifest in the flesh, justified in the Spirit, seen of angels, preached unto the Gentiles, believed on in the world, received up into glory" (1 Timothy 3:16 KJV).

This dual nature is seen in the Torah during the destruction of Sodom and Gomorrah. Genesis 19:24 reads: *"Then the LORD (YHVH) rained upon Sodom and upon Gomorrah brimstone and fire from the LORD (YHVH) out of heaven;"* (KJV).

In this passage context the word "Lord" (YHVH) is in two places: Earth and Heaven. The ancient rabbis taught that the Lord on Earth was the Angel of the Lord. However, reason and the Hebrew language say it could not be the case.

Yeshua - Your Lasting Ladder

The third way reveals Yeshua to be your *lasting* ladder. Other ladders wear out with use, but this ladder lasts forever.

Yeshua, by his obedience to God as your representative and covenant surety, is your everlasting righteousness:

"Seventy 'sevens' are decreed for your people and your holy city to finish transgression, to put an end to sin, to atone for wickedness, to bring in everlasting righteousness, to seal up vision and prophecy and to anoint the most holy" (Daniel 9:24 NIV).

The redemption He accomplished for you is an eternal redemption:

"But when the Messiah appeared as Cohen Gadol of the good things that are happening already, then, through the greater and more perfect Tent which is not man-made (that is, it is not of this created world)" (Hebrews 9:12 CJB).

The salvation He gives to you is an eternal salvation:

"And after he had been brought to the goal, he became the source of eternal deliverance to all who obey him" (Hebrews 5:9 CJB).

Yeshua - Your Free Ladder

The fourth way reveals Yeshua to be your *free* Ladder. All who come are welcome. The promise of the gospel is proclaimed in broad general terms:

"Come to me, all of you who are struggling and burdened, and I will give you rest" (Matthew 11:28 CJB).

Additional reference Scriptures can be found in John 7:37 and Revelation 22:17. Yeshua is the "Door Opened" to God and His grace, not the "Door Closed." If you do not exclude yourself by unbelief, God will not exclude you.

Yeshua - Your Firm Ladder

The fifth way reveals Yeshua to be your *firm* Ladder. You can stand on this ladder without fear of falling. Hebrews 2:9-11 reads:

"But we do see Yeshua - who indeed was made for a little while lower than the angels - now crowned with glory and honor because he suffered death, so that by God's grace he might taste death for all humanity. For in bringing many sons to glory, it was only fitting that God, the Creator and Preserver of everything, should bring the Initiator of their deliverance to the goal through sufferings."

For both Yeshua, who sets people apart for God, and the ones being set apart have a common origin - this is why he is not ashamed to call them brothers" (CJB).

Yeshua saves all His people completely from their sins. He saves His people from the guilt of sin, the dominion of sin, the penalty of sin, the consequences of sin, and even from the actual being of sin by His power.

Yeshua - Your Fitted Ladder

The sixth and last way reveals Yeshua to be your *fitted* ladder. There is no other way to God. Out of all the religions in the world, only one has a Messiah. It is Judaism, from which Messianic Judaism and Christianity came into being. Many people say there are many ladders, but God says, "The Jewish Messiah is the ladder." The Scriptures read,

"Yeshua [my translation] saith unto him, I am the way, the truth, and the life: no man cometh unto the Father, but by me" (John 14:6 KJV).

This ladder must be climbed to receive all the benefits. If any other ladder is used, you will find when you get to the top that your ladder was placed on the wrong building. This brings you to the question:

HOW DO YOU CLIMB THE LADDER?

How do you climb the ladder? You do it by trust through faith. Faith is the hand by which you take hold of your ladder, and trust, through faith, is the feet by which you climb.

"But without faith it is impossible to please him: for he that cometh to God must believe that he is, and that he is a rewarder of them that diligently seek him" (Hebrews 11:6 KJV).

Trust increases and faith grows by an action moved by love, not fear or indifference. You learn to climb the ladder of trust by climbing another ladder. It is the ladder of your walk

"And beside this, giving all diligence, add to your faith virtue; and to virtue knowledge; And to knowledge temperance; and to temperance patience; and to patience Godliness; And to Godliness brotherly kindness; and to brotherly kindness charity" (2 Peter 1:5-7 KJV).

There are eight rungs to the ladder of your walk. Starting with the first, named faith, you go up through virtue, knowledge, temperance, patience, godliness, brotherly kindness, and the last rung, charity or love.

Please notice: you start the climb of this ladder of your walk through faith. You cannot come into God's kingdom, God's presence, or God's glory but by the Jewish Messiah.

The only way any of your performances can go up to God as a "sweet savor" is by the way of the Messiah, Yeshua - your ladder. Your performance must begin, and continue, by faith.

"Ye also, as lively stones, are built up a spiritual house, an holy priesthood, to offer up spiritual sacrifices, accept-

able to God by <u>*Yeshua the Messiah*</u> *[my translation]"* (1 Peter 2:5 KJV).

According to the Scriptures, the "spiritual sacrifices" are a "living sacrifice" – your body:

"I beseech you therefore, brethren, by the mercies of God, that ye present your bodies a living sacrifice, holy, acceptable unto God, which is your reasonable service. And be not conformed to this world: but be ye transformed by the renewing of your mind, that ye may prove what is that good, and acceptable, and perfect, will of God" (Romans 12:1-2 KJV).

How do you present your body as a "living sacrifice"? The answer is through obedience.

"Now that no man is justified by the law before God, is evident: for, the righteous shall live by faith;"

"and the law (Torah) is not of faith; but, He that doeth them shall live in them" (Galatians 3:11-12 KJV).

The covenant of Moses is not a faith covenant. It is based on obedience. It is not a covenant of promise, but it protects what you already have.

Obedience is not done for rewards or from fear. It is done because God says so, and is done from love. Obedience flows out of trust. The trust produces faith that is enjoyed and expressed. Your attitude keeps your worship from becoming a works program.

"BEHOLD THE LADDER"

The distance between earth and heaven is infinite, producing a long uphill climb. How do you get there? The answer is: behold the ladder.

You count, in two ways, the rungs of the ladder. The first way is from the top down, as according to scripture, Yeshua came down to you. The second way is from the bottom up, as according to Scripture, you - in Yeshua - are reaching up to God.

You count these rungs with your past experience by four ways. First, you receive faith in Yeshua. Second, you are born of God and called by His Spirit. Third, all who are called by His Spirit are redeemed and justified. And fourth, you are glorified by His grace according to God's purpose.

In Romans, the Scripture lays this groundwork:

"And you know that all things work together for good to them that love God, to them who are the called according to his purpose. For whom he did foreknow, he also did predestinate to be conformed to the image of his Son, that he might be the firstborn among many brethren."

"Moreover whom he did predestinate, them he also called: and whom he called, them he also justified: and whom he justified, them he also glorified" (Romans 8:28-30 KJV).

Every ladder has two sidepieces connecting the rungs, giving it strength and stability. Side one is God's eternal purpose. Side two is God's preserving grace. The word "behold" suggests something you are responsible to do. You are to *"behold the ladder,"* and bless God for it.

There are four special times when you behold your Ladder, Yeshua. The first time is when you attempt to do anything for God. Yeshua must be your strength, your guide and your acceptance.

"ADONAI will always guide you; he will satisfy your needs in the desert, he will renew the strength in your limbs; so that you will be like a watered garden, like a spring whose water never fails" (Isaiah 58:11 CJB).

Psalm 23 tells you that He will guide you like a shepherd.

The second time is when you did anything wrong against God. John, the apostle, wrote in 1 John 2:1-2:

"My little children, these things write I unto you, that ye sin not. And if any man sin, you have an advocate with the Father, <u>Yeshua the Messiah</u> [my translation] the righteous:

And he is the propitiation for your sins: and not for yours only, but also for the sins of the whole world" (1 John 2:1-2 KJV).

This comes because of guilt facing you. When it happens, God is telling you these words:

"I will cleanse them from all their sins, through which they offended me; and I will pardon all their sins, through which they offended and rebelled against me" (Jeremiah 33:8 CJB).

When you need pardon, cleansing, and reviving, you should *"behold the ladder."*

The third time is when you are facing distress, trouble, or danger: The Esaus of this world, wanting to harm you, surround you. Your example in this circumstance is King David who wrote these words: *"In my anguish I cried to the Lord, and he answered by setting me free"* (Psalm 118:5 NIV). Like David, this situation also moves you to *"behold the ladder."*

The fourth and last time is when you are facing your final fear: death. The ladder of Yeshua becomes a lifeline for you, not a crutch. Remember Stephen's battle cry? What caused the religious leaders to attack Stephen with vengeance? What caused Paul to go after the Messianic Jewish believers, starting the very same day after Stephen's death?

When a king or government official was hearing a case presented before him, He would be seated. At the point when He was ready to pronounce judgment, He will do it by standing. The religious leaders during Yeshua's time would have known these Scriptures:

"For the leader. A psalm of David. A song:

Let God arise [emphasis mine]*, let his enemies be scattered; let those who hate him flee from his presence. Drive them away as smoke is driven away; like wax melting in the presence of a fire, let the wicked perish in the presence of*

God. But let the righteous rejoice and be glad in God's presence; yes, let them Exult and rejoice" (Psalms 68:1-3 CJB).

Stephen, the deacon, before the Sanhedrin, proclaimed God's judgment on the leaders (Acts 7:51-53) because of the sins of the people. He was rejected and stoned. At the point of dying, Scripture records Stephen's last words:

*"And said, Behold, I see the heavens opened, and the Son of man **standing** [emphasis mine] on the right hand of God."* (Acts 7:56 KJV)

Stephen left no doubt in the minds of the leaders as to who the "Son of Man" was. He knew something that most people never discover. There is nothing worth living for, unless it is worth dying for.

At your time of dying, let this be your battle cry: "BEHOLD THE LADDER!"

III. THE NOACHIDE COMMANDMENTS

"Faith is different from proof; the latter is human, the former is a Gift from God"
Blaise Pascal (1623-1662)

III. THE NOACHIDE COMMANDMENTS

=≪∞≫=

"Don't you know that you yourselves are God's temple and that God's Spirit lives in you? If anyone destroys God's temple, God will destroy him; for God's temple is sacred, and you are that temple." **(1 Corinthians 3:16 - 17 NIV)**

THE SEVEN LAWS

An understanding of the Noachide Commandments is required to comprehend the qualifications of the Gentile to live in the land. The Noachide commandments consist of seven commandments: six negative precepts, one positive.

There are a number of Gentile groups, called "B'nai Noach," that follow the seven laws of Noah as stated by the Jewish rabbis. These Gentile groups try to apply these seven laws to Act 15:20, but can it be done? Where did the seven laws come from?

Rabbi Yochanan explains the Noachide Law in the Talmud. The understanding of the first six Noachide Laws comes from the Hebrew of Genesis 2:16. It reads in Hebrew and English as follows: "VAYITSAV HASHEM ELOKIM

AL HAADM LEIMOR MICHAL EITS HAGAN OCHEL,"
which translates to, "*And Hashem God commanded the man,
saying, of every tree of the garden you may freely eat.*"

There is much speculation and disagreement as to what
is part of the Noachide Law, even among Jewish scholars. A
number of rabbinic sources during the ages took these seven
laws and subdivided them into thirty-two laws.

The First Law - Idolatry

The first law is the prohibition against idolatry. Idolatry
is forbidden. Man is commanded to believe in the One God
alone and worship only Him. The Hebrew word, "tsav"
(command) is connected to Hosea 5:11:

"*Ephraim is oppressed, he is crushed in judgment;
because he was content to walk after man's command (tsav)*"
(ASV).

"Tsav" is a reference to the worship of idols. In this
verse, the word "tsav" is used in reference to people doing
the command (tsav). The "commandment," which "Ephraim
willingly went after," was the idolatry of Jeroboam.

From this first commandment, two additional commandments were added. They are: pray only to God, and offer
ritual sacrifices only to God.

The Second Law - Blasphemy

The second law is the prohibition against blasphemy.
Cursing the name of God is forbidden.

Besides honoring and respecting God, this precept teaches
you that your speech must be sanctified. Why? Speech is the
distinctive sign that God gave us and that He used to separate man from the animals.

The Hebrew word "*Hashem*" (God) used in Leviticus
24:16 and the prohibition against cursing God recorded in
this verse are connected. Leviticus 24:16 also use the name
"*Hashem*":

"And whoever blasphemes the name of the Lord [Hashem] shall surely be put to death. All the congregation shall certainly stone him, the stranger as well as him who is born in the land. When he blasphemes the name of the Lord [Hashem], he shall be put to death" (KJV).

Again, this second commandment was subdivided into another additional ten commandments. They are: believe in the singularity on God, no witchcraft, no divination, no conjurers, no sorcerers, no mediums, no demonology, no wizardry, no necromancy, and to honor your father and mother.

The Third Law - Murder

The third law is the prohibition against murder. Murder is forbidden. The life of a human being, formed in God's image, is sacred. The Hebrew word, "Al HaAdam" meaning "to the man," also refers to the command against murder recorded in Genesis 9:6. The word "Adam," used to describe man, is in this verse.

"Whoever sheds man's blood, by man [adam] his blood shall be shed; for in the image of God He made man [adam]" (ASV).

Under this third commandment, three additional commandments were added. They are: no suicide, no infant sacrifice (also known as *"Moloch worship"*), and no abortion. The *"no abortion"* commandment was placed in this list by the Jewish rabbi, Maimonides, also called "the *Rambam*," who lived in Spain during the middle ages.

The Fourth Law – Sexual Immorality

The fourth law is the prohibition on sexual immorality. Incestuous and adulterous relations are forbidden. Human beings are not sex objects, nor are pleasures the ultimate goal of life.

The Hebrew word, "leimor" (saying) connects this verse and Jeremiah 3:1, which starts with the word "Leimor." Jeremiah 3:1 discusses sexually immoral acts.

"They say (LEIMOR), 'If a man put away his wife, and she go from him, and becomes another man's, shall he return unto her again?' shall not that land be greatly polluted? but thou hast played the harlot with many lovers; yet return again to Me,' saith the Lord" (KJV).

The Middle Ages rabbis took this commandment of sexual immorality and subdivided it into seven commandments. They were: no adultery, no incest with close relatives, no sodomy, no bestiality, no crossbreeding animals, no castration, and no sex before you have a formal marriage.

The Fifth Law - Theft

The fifth law is the prohibition against theft. The world is not ours to do with as we please. The Jewish rabbis took this law from the plain meaning of the verses in Genesis 2:16-17. They gave Adam the right to eat from the trees of the garden, except for one tree.

"And the Lord God commanded the man, saying, "Of every tree of the garden thou mayest freely eat;"

"but of the tree of the knowledge of good and evil, thou shalt not eat of it: for in the day that thou eatest thereof thou shalt surely die." (KJV).

Adam was forbidden to eat from the tree of the knowledge of good and evil because the property did not belong to him.

From this fifth commandment, the ancient rabbis added another one: no kidnapping of persons.

The Sixth Law – Establish Laws And Courts

The sixth law is the command for mankind to establish laws and courts of justice.

A just social order is needed to enforce the six laws and enact any other useful laws or customs. The Hebrew word, *"Elokim"* (God) connects Exodus 21:6, which uses that name in referring to judges:

"Then his master shall bring him unto the judges [Elokim]; he shall also bring him to the door, or unto the doorpost; and his master shall bore his ear through with an awl; and he shall serve him forever" (KJV).

Under this system of justice, the commandment of no false oaths was added.

The Seventh Law – Eating Flesh With Blood

The seventh law is the prohibition against eating the limb of a living animal. You may not eat flesh with its blood, which is its life. This teaches you to be sensitive to cruelty to animals. (This commandment was given to Noah for the first time along with the permission of eating meat. The rest were already given to Adam in the Garden of Eden.) This comes from the plain meaning of Genesis 9:4 (ASV). God is talking to Noah when He says:

"But flesh with the life thereof, [which is] the blood thereof, shall ye not eat."

The rabbis added two additional commandments to this seventh law. They are: no eating or drinking blood, and no eating the carcass of a dead animal, called *"carrion"* by a Jewish court of law.

These seven laws and its subdivisions were for the Gentiles in their midst. What is the problem that connects the Gentiles to the Noachide commandments?

The Time Frame Problem

The earliest Jewish written record for these laws can be found in the Jewish writings called the Tosefta (supplement) under *"Avoda Zera 8:4."* It reads as follows:

"Concerning seven requirements were the children of Noah admonished: setting up courts of justice, idolatry, blasphemy, fornication, bloodshed, thievery, and a limb from a living animal." [7]

Another Jewish writing called the Bavli, also known as the Babylonian Talmud, in the tractate *"Sanhedrin 58b,"* also gives the same list of these laws. Jewish rabbis used these writings to show that a Gentile, if he or she lived by these laws, would be considered a "righteous Gentile." The Gentile would become part of the world to come by applying these "Noachide Laws" in his life. There is a problem with that understanding.

The Tosefta was codified roughly around 300C.E. The Bavli was codified around 500 C.E. What does that mean? This shows that a precise formation of the Noachide Laws was still being debated as late as 300 – 500 C.E. [8] It also shows the rabbinic formulation of the Noachide Laws did not occur until about two hundred fifty years after the time of the apostles. Even at this time, there was no record that Gentiles would be considered righteous by obeying them. This teaching would come from Rabbi Moshe ben Maimon (Rambam), who was born in 1135 C.E., and is found in his *"Mishneh Torah: Sefer Shoftim."*

"Anyone who accepts upon himself the fulfillment of these seven mitzvot and is precise in their observance is considered one of the 'pious among the gentiles' and will merit a share in the World to come." [9]

The last *"Bet Din"* recorded in Scripture is found with the Jerusalem Council in Acts 15. In this council, four commandments were given to the Gentiles. They are found in Acts 15:20: *"But that we write unto them, that they abstain from pollutions of idols, and from fornication, and from what is strangled, and from blood"* (ASV).

Proving that these four commandments are part of the Noachide Laws for the Gentiles, because of this time frame, would have its problems. Proving that these four commandments in Acts are part of the Torah for Gentiles to follow for living in the land is not.

THE GENTILE COMMANDMENTS

Before we continue, a point must be made. When a teaching is given which disagrees with the doctrine that was taught, it could be misinterpreted as church bashing. This is not the case, nor is it my intention. It is to supply, you, the reader, with an understanding of the context of the Scriptures.

Any Gentile who wanted to live in the land at the time of Yeshua had to perform the Gentile commandments of the Torah.

"Therefore it is my judgment that we do not trouble those who are turning to God from among the Gentiles but that we write to them that they abstain from things contaminated by idols and from fornication and from what is strangled and from blood."

"For Moses from ancient generations has in every city those who preach him, since he is read in the synagogues every Sabbath" (Acts 15:19-21 ASV).

If the Gentiles only had four commandments to follow, what did Jacob, also known as James, mean by the last verse? Two conclusions can be understood: First, Gentiles were expected to enter the Synagogues to hear the Torah (God's instructions), and to be instructed in the ways of God. And second, the Lord's Sabbath was to be observed by these Gentiles along with the Jews as it is commanded in the Torah.

*"But the seventh day is the Sabbath of the LORD thy God: in it thou shalt not do any work, thou, nor thy son, nor thy daughter, thy manservant, nor thy maidservant, nor thy cattle, **nor thy stranger** [emphasis mine] that is within thy gates"* (Exodus 20:10 KJV).

For those who would disagree, two questions must be answered: Has God created a double standard between the Jew and the Gentile? If He did, how does that produce one new man?

It is totally unbiblical to believe that there are two different types, or classes, of believers following two different sets of laws.

The doctrine showing one law strictly for the Jewish believers based on the Torah, and the other law for the Gentile believers based on grace without the Torah (Exodus 12:49, Leviticus 18:26, Numbers 15:16) is not scriptural. Grace has always existed for both the Jewish and Gentile believers.

The four commandments given to the Gentile, and passed by the Acts 15 *"Bet Din,"* were part of the Torah for Gentiles given to Moses by God. Jacob (James) announced that Gentiles who accept Yeshua as their Jewish Messiah would not be forced into circumcision. They would be required to abstain only from four activities: eating meat sacrificed to idols, engaging in sexual immorality, eating the meat of strangled animals, and consuming blood. All four commandments listed can be found between Leviticus 17:1 – 18:30. Let's look at these four commandments:

Eating Meat Sacrificed To Idols (Acts 15:20)

The first commandment listed is "eating meat sacrificed to idols." A special Greek word is used to describe this commandment. The Greek word *"al-is-ghem-ah"* is only listed one time in Scripture: here. Its literal meaning is "contaminated, pollution, condemnation." The reference in the Torah for this commandment is found in Leviticus 17:3-9:

"What man soever there be of the house of Israel, that killeth an ox, or lamb, or goat, in the camp, or that killeth it without the camp, and hath not brought it unto the door of the tent of meeting, to offer it as an oblation unto Adonai

[my translation] before the tabernacle of <u>Adonai</u> [my translation]: blood shall be imputed unto that man;"

"he hath shed blood; and that man shall be cut off from among his people: To the end that the children of Israel may bring their sacrifices, which they sacrifice in the open field, even that they may bring them unto <u>Adonai</u>[my translation], unto the door of the tent of meeting, unto the priest, and sacrifice them for sacrifices of peace-offerings unto <u>Adonai</u> [my translation]."

"And the priest shall sprinkle the blood upon the altar of <u>Adonai</u>[my translation] at the door of the tent of meeting, and burn the fat for a sweet savor unto <u>Adonai</u> [my translation]. And they shall no more sacrifice their sacrifices unto the he-goats, after which they play the harlot. This shall be a statute forever unto them throughout their generations."

"And thou shalt say unto them, Whatsoever man there be of the house of Israel, **or of the strangers that sojourn among them** *[emphasis mine], that offereth a burnt-offering or sacrifice, and bringeth it not unto the door of the tent of meeting, to sacrifice it unto <u>Adonai</u> [my translation]; that man shall be cut off from his people"* (KJV).

The Scriptures required the Gentile to bring the ox, lamb, or goat to the tabernacle, the tent of meeting. One of the sacrifices was the peace offering, in which part of this sacrifice was to be eaten. The sacrifices Gentiles made to idols were actually sacrifices made to demons according to the Scriptures (1 Corinthians 10:19-21):

"So, what am I saying? That food sacrificed to idols has any significance in itself? or that an idol has significance in itself?"

"No, what I am saying is that the things which pagans sacrifice, they sacrifice not to God but to demons; and I don't want you to become sharers of the demons!"

"You can't drink both a cup of the Lord and a cup of demons, you can't partake in both a meal of the Lord and a meal of demons" (CJB).

James' command was designed for three purposes: to remove this demonic influence from the lives of the Gentiles coming in to the assembly of Israel, to open the door to the Gentiles for table fellowship with their Jewish believers, and the Gentiles to obey the Torah as it relates to them.

Engaging In Sexual Immorality (Acts 15:20)

The second commandment given by Jacob (James) is against "engaging in sexual immorality."

The references for these Torah commandments can be found in Leviticus 18:6-23 and Deuteronomy 22:23-29. They include homosexuality (Leviticus.18:22, 20:13), incest (Leviticus 18:1-18), rape (Deuteronomy 22:23-29), adultery (Exodus 19:14; Leviticus 18:20; Deuteronomy 22:22), bestiality (Leviticus 18:23, 20:15), premarital sex (Deuteronomy 22:23-29), and sex with a woman during the time of her uncleanness (Leviticus 18:19).

Now read Revelation 2:14; 22:14-15:

"But I have a few things against thee, because thou hast there some that hold the teaching of Balaam, who taught Balak to cast a stumbling block before the children of Israel, **to eat things sacrificed to idols, and to commit fornication** [emphasis mine]."

"Blessed are they that wash their robes, that they may have the right to come to the tree of life, and may enter in by the gates into the city. Without are the dogs, and the sorcerers, and **the fornicators** [emphasis mine], *and the murderers, and* **the idolaters** [emphasis mine], *and every one that loveth and maketh a lie"* (KJV).

Why are these verses important? It cannot be said that it does not apply now. The above commandments are connected to this list in the book of Revelation. It also means that if the book of Revelation was written between 90-100 C.E., then paganism and idolatry already had corrupted the church.

Eating the Meat of Strangled Animals (Acts 15:20)

The third commandment given by Jacob (James) is *"eating the meat of strangled animals."* This commandment literally means "deprived of life without the shedding of blood," and is based on the Torah as recorded in Leviticus 17:12-16:

*"Therefore I said unto the children of Israel, No soul of you shall eat blood, **neither shall any stranger that sojourneth among you** [emphasis mine] eat blood."*

*"And whatsoever man there be of the children of Israel, **or of the strangers that sojourn among them** [emphasis mine], who taketh in hunting any beast or bird that may be eaten; he shall pour out the blood thereof, and cover it with dust."*

"For as to the life of all flesh, the blood thereof is all one with the life thereof: therefore, I said unto the children of Israel, Ye shall eat the blood of no manner of flesh;"

"for the life of all flesh is the blood thereof: whosoever eateth it shall be cut off."

*"And every soul that eateth that which dieth of itself, or that which is torn of beasts, whether he be home-born **or a sojourner** [emphasis mine], he shall wash his clothes, and bathe himself in water, and be unclean until the even: then shall he be clean. But if he wash them not, nor bathe his flesh, then he shall bear his iniquity"* (KJV).

Why is this important? Leviticus 11:44-45 gives the answer. It states:

"For I am the LORD your God: ye shall therefore sanctify yourselves, and ye shall be holy; for I am holy: neither shall ye defile yourselves with any manner of creeping thing that creepeth upon the earth."

"For I am the LORD that bringeth you up out of the land of Egypt, to be your God: ye shall therefore be holy, for I am holy" (KJV).

Ezekiel 44 talks about the future temple during the millennium. Let's look at these verses:

"They are to teach my people the difference between the holy and the common and show them how to distinguish between the unclean and the clean" (Ezekiel 44:23 NIV).

"The priests must not eat anything, bird or animal, found dead or torn by wild animals" (Ezekiel 44:31 NIV).

Isaiah 66:17-18 is also connected to the Millennium:

"'Those who consecrate and purify themselves to go into the gardens, following the one in the midst of those who eat the flesh of pigs and rats and other abominable things—they will meet their end together,' declares the Lord."

"And I, because of their actions and their imaginations, am about to come and gather all nations and tongues, and they will come and see my glory" (NIV).

These verses show a biblical kosher concept, which according to Scripture will exist in the Millennium. Why is this important? It forces you to answer the question: if God wants you to be holy in the Torah and in the Millennium, then who changed the middle? (See the history in Appendix 4).

Consuming Blood (Acts 15:20)

The fourth commandment given to the Gentiles by Jacob (James) is against "consuming blood." In the *Brit Hadashah*, the Greek word for blood, *"heh'-ee-mah,"* is listed ninety-nine times. A better understanding would be the Hebrew word, *"dam."*

In the Tanakh this Hebrew word is listed three hundred sixty-two times, of which two hundred three times refer to death or violence, one hundred three times to the blood of the sacrifices, seven times connected to life and blood, seventeen times linking eating meat with blood, and thirty-two times with no connection. These numbers show that when a Jewish person hears the word "*blood*," he associates it with death.

The reference for this fourth commandment is found in Leviticus 17:10-14:

"*And whatsoever man there be of the house of Israel, **or of the strangers that sojourn** [emphasis mine] among them, that eateth any manner of blood, I will set my face against that soul that eateth blood, and will cut him off from among his people. For the life of the flesh is in the blood; and I have given it to you upon the altar to make atonement for your souls: for it is the blood that maketh atonement by reason of the life.*"

" *Therefore, I said unto the children of Israel, No soul of you shall eat blood, **neither shall any stranger that sojourneth among you** [emphasis mine] eat blood.*"

"*And whatsoever man there be of the children of Israel, or **of the strangers that sojourn**_[emphasis mine] among them, who taketh in hunting any beast or bird that may be eaten; he shall pour out the blood thereof, and cover it with dust.*"

"*For as to the life of all flesh, the blood thereof is all one with the life thereof: therefore I said unto the children of Israel, Ye shall eat the blood of no manner of flesh; for the life of all flesh is the blood thereof: whosoever eateth it shall be cut off*" (KJV).

The blood, which refers to the Seat of Life, has two meanings. Its context determines the meaning: It could be the blood of animals or man. In this situation, it is the blood of an animal.

So serious was this principle that it became one of the three times in recorded scriptures where God will "*set His face against that man*" for engaging in a specific sin. The additional two places are Leviticus 20:2-5 for Idol Worship, and Leviticus 20:6 for seeking after familiar spirits and wizards.

WHY FOLLOW THE FOUR COMMANDMENTS?

Since the complete Law of Moses was not in question, Jacob's (James) judgment could not have abolished the Torah in favor of the four requirements he gave to Gentiles. If substitution was his intention, he left a lot of holes in his replacement law code. He left out murder, theft and many other uncivilized actions prohibited in the Torah and condemned in the *Brit Hadashah*.

Simple logic says these four requirements were not all the laws Gentiles were expected to follow as believers in Yeshua.

Why did Jacob's (James) address only those four? The answer is in the next verse:

"For Moses from generations of old hath in every city them that preach him, being read in the synagogues every Sabbath" (Acts 15:21 KJV).

By abstaining from these pagan practices, the Gentiles would be ritualistically clean enough to enter the synagogues every Sabbath.

Once in the synagogue, they would hear Moses, and be exposed to the Torah that God would put *"in their minds"* and write *"on their hearts,"* thereby fulfilling Ezekiel 36:26-27:

"A new heart also will I give you, and a new spirit will I put within you; and I will take away the stony heart out of your flesh, and I will give you a heart of flesh."

"And I will put my Spirit within you, and cause you to walk in my statutes, and ye shall keep mine ordinances, and do them" (KJV).

This above verse is repeated in Hebrews 8:8-10 and in Hebrews 10:16. It allows you to see two observations: first, the renewed covenant is the writing of Torah on your heart.

In the renewed covenant, you are not under the law because it has been internalized. You do it out of the love of God, not to get "brownie points" with God. It is the wrong motive. It is also not to "get saved." You are saved.

Second, the renewed covenant was made with the house of Israel, not with Gentiles. What does this tell you? Anti-Semitism cannot exist in the heart of a converted Gentile in the body of Messiah.

Acts 15 is one of the most misunderstood chapters in the Scriptures. Acts 15:21 has been widely taught in error because of the "*anti-torah*" bias in its interpretation. Many people use this chapter to claim that the Torah given to Moses was nullified and no longer apply to the new covenant Gentile believer. The *Encyclopedia Britannica* reflects this understanding, saying:

"The Jerusalem Council was a conference of believers and Apostles in Jerusalem at about 50 C.E., which decreed that Gentile Believers did not have to observe the Mosaic law of the Jews."

Is this true? No, it is not. The context does not allow it. There were two camps at the "*Bet Din*." The first camp was known as the pro-circumcision advocates, as recorded in Acts15:5. The second camp was known as the anti-circumcision advocates, as recorded in Acts 15:2-4, 7-18.

The debate in this chapter was on circumcision, not the Mosaic law of the Jews.

There is also a misconception that only Jews attended the synagogues, but the book of Acts shows that Gentiles were also present (Acts 13:14-32; 14:1; 17:1-4, 10-12, 17; 18:8). If you keep in mind that Jacob (James) is explaining the reason for his decision to not require circumcision from adult Gentile males, as well as the reason for the four commandments he did put on the Gentiles, this verse makes sense.

Jacob (James) was answering the Pharisee's earlier contention that it was necessary to circumcise the Gentiles in order *"to instruct and to keep the Law of Moses"*(Acts 15: 5). He is stating that the Gentile who is attending the Sabbath services can accomplish this same goal, and that these four requirements would allow it to happen. With this understanding, would come obedience.

The Gentile living in the land would learn Leviticus 12:1-3, and would understand that it was required that his male children be circumcised on the eighth day in order to follow the Torah.

Before closing this chapter, a question must be answered because of the *"anti-torah"* bias attached to the chapter of Acts 15. In verse 10, Peter makes this statement:

"So why do you test God by putting on the disciples' neck a yoke that neither our ancestors nor we could carry?"

What "yoke" was Peter talking about?

"Anti-Torah" Bible teachers teach that the "yoke" is the Torah. This can only be true if you take the scriptures out of context. Only one issue is discussed here, circumcision, not the Law of Moses.

Peter's reference to a "yoke" referred to circumcision. By his question: "Why do you test God?" Peter rebuked those who wanted to require the circumcision of adult Gentile converts

The last 2 verbs, translated "were able to bear," are in the aorist tense! In Greek, it means that the action was a *one-time* event, again eliminating that it was the complete Torah. It meant that the Jew would have to be physically strong to bear it, and gives an understanding of pain on the adult, Jew or Gentile.

The best Scripture to close out this chapter is found in 1 Corinthians 6:19–20:

"Do you not know that your body is a temple of the Ruach Hakodesh [my translation], who is in you, whom you have

received from God? You are not your own; you were bought at a price. Therefore honor God with your body" (NIV).

IV. FOUR TYPES OF GENTILES

"Faith without reason leads to superstition:
Reason without faith leads to cynicism."

Anonymous

IV. FOUR TYPES OF GENTILES

———

> *"He who turns away his ear from listening to the law, even his prayer is an abomination."* **(Proverbs 28:9 ASV)**

WHICH GROUP FITS YOU?

"And a highway shall be there, and a way, and it shall be called The Holy Way; the clean unclean shall not pass over it; but it shall be for the Redeemed; the wayfaring men, yes, the simple ones and fools, shall not err in it or lose their way. No lion shall be there, nor shall any ravenous beast come up on it; they shall not be found there; but the redeemed shall walk on it. And the ransomed of the Lord shall return, and come to Zion with singing, and everlasting joy shall be upon their heads; they shall obtain joy and gladness, and sorrow and sighing shall flee away" (Isaiah 35:8-10 AMP).

There was a dividing wall in the Temple, which separated the Gentiles from the rest of the Temple. The wall is no longer in place. If you are a Jew, it was not for you to escape, but to come near. This process also allows the Gentiles to come near.

If you are a Gentile, your walk on the highway of holiness begins with an understanding of the four types of Gentiles recorded in Scripture. Faith and reason determine your type. The Bible says you move *"from faith to faith"* (Romans 1:17 KJV). This process moves you up the ladder of trust, and through the four types of Gentiles.

The first chapter of this book laid down the two end result foundational concepts. They are: Yeshua was - and is - Jewish, and the Scriptures are Jewish, not Gentile. These concepts apply to how you look at the Word of God.

Great care must be undertaken for the meaning of words in the original languages of the Bible: Hebrew and Greek. The word "Gentile" in Hebrew is *"goyim."* In Greek, the word is *"ethos."* It is God's shorthand for the seventy nations. Who are the four types of Gentiles recorded in Scripture?

THE PAGAN

The first type of *"goyim"* in Scriptures is considered an idolater, the wicked, or the pagan. In Hebrew, they are also known as *"Nochri,"* Gentiles who did not observe the Gentile laws of the Torah. All *goyim* who were ignorant of the God of Israel are part of this group. According to Scripture, they have no covenant with God. The Scripture says:

"You have been made dead because of your sins and acts of disobedience. You walked in the ways of the 'olam hazeh' (this world) and obeyed the Ruler of the Powers of the Air, who is still at work among the disobedient."

" Indeed, we all once lived this way – we followed the passions of our old nature and obeyed the wishes of our old nature and our own thoughts."

" In the natural condition we were headed for God's wrath, just like everyone else at that time had no Messiah. You were estranged from the national life of Israel. You were foreigners to the covenants embodying God's promise. You

were in this world without hope and without God" (Ephesians 2:1-3,12 CJB).

You cannot go where God wants you to go by taking an alternate route. God moves in the world through His covenant. The covenant with God can either be a privilege or an obligation, depending upon your attitude and understanding of what counts most in life.

What does it mean if you are not under a covenant? People do not like to hear about the fire and brimstone of Hell. They can, by creating their own doctrine, dismiss Hell as a fantasy, but there are more scriptures dealing with the afterlife than there is with Gentile repentance.

If you are this type of Gentile, the scriptures say where you stand. On June 8, 1741, Jonathan Edwards used these Scriptures for the first time in his sermon, *"Sinners in the hands of an angry God."* The following information is a paraphrase, in my words, from parts of this sermon.

"Consider this: only the pleasure of God keeps you out of hell. God does not lack the power to send you to hell (Luke 12:4-5), and because of God's divine justice, you deserve to be cast into hell. Only God's mercies and grace will hold back the judgment.

Here is another point. According to Scripture, you are already under a sentence of condemnation to hell (John 3:18). You are the object of the anger and wrath of God. What does Scripture say about the fierceness of the anger you are exposed to?

"According to their deeds, so He will repay, wrath to his adversaries, recompense to His enemies; to the coastlands He will make recompense" (Isaiah 59:18 - ASV)

"And from His mouth comes a sharp sword, so that with it He may smite the nations; and he will rule them with a rod of iron and he treads the wine press of the fierce wrath of God the Almighty" (Revelation 19:15 ASV).

God holds you in His hand, and nothing but the mere pleasure of God, an angry God with an everlasting wrath, is protecting you. The devil is ready to receive you. You are his goods. He owns you by right, and wants you in hell. You have no security and no visible means to protect yourself from death except the will of God, and He is angry with you. Remember what God called the person who had no concern about Him?

"But God said to him, 'You Fool! This very night your soul is required of you; and now who will own what you have prepared?" (Luke 12:20 ASV)

You can flatter yourself, depending on your own security, by believing that what you are now doing or will do will keep you from damnation. You will be deluding yourself by placing your confidence in your own strength and wisdom.

You can do many good deeds, but without being in a covenant it will not help. Good deeds will not keep you out of hell. Like a rock going through a spider's web, your good deeds will not stop your descent into hell. Like sand moving through an hourglass, there comes a time when your life on earth will stop.

Once you step into hell, God will not have mercy to remove you from it. A million years later, you will still be in the fire and pain of hell. God will still be angry with you, and the devil will not let you go.

Only one thing can stop the pain. You must be under a covenant with God before this point is reached. If not, the Scripture says, *"It is a terrifying thing to fall into the hands of the living God"* (Hebrews 10:31 ASV)." [10]

It is my heartfelt prayer that you remove yourself from this condition and place yourself under God's covenant.

"I call on heaven and earth to witness against you today that I have presented you with life and death, the blessing and the curse."

"Therefore, choose life, so that you will live, you and your descendants, loving ADONAI your God, paying attention to what he says and clinging to him - for that is the purpose of your life! On this depends the length of time you will live in the land ADONAI swore he would give to your ancestors Avraham, Yitz'chak and Ya'akov" (Deuteronomy 30:19-20 CJB).

Pascal's Wager

Blaise Pascal was born on June 19, 1623 and died August 19, 1662. He was thirty-nine years old when he died of cancer. Pascal, during his short life, was known as a great mathematician. In 1654, he created what is known as "Pascal's Triangle," which calculated the probabilities of winning in gambling and is used today in the study of statistics and modern day physics.

Four years before the end of his life, he gave it all up because he found a question that occupied his entire thinking process: Does God exist? He believed that every person lives his life in this world based on his or her belief in the afterlife. God exists or He does not exist, and you must, from necessity, lay odds for or against Him. His conclusion became known as "Pascal's Wager."

The wager goes like this: If you believe that God exists, live your life on the basis of my belief, and die, your choice is made. If you were wrong, and God did not exist, you have not lost anything. If you were right, and God does exist, you have gained everything.

If you believe that God does not exist, live your life on the basis of that belief, and die, your choice is made. If you are right, and God does not exist, you have gained nothing. If you are wrong, and God does exist, you have lost everything.

History records Pascal's choice. What is yours? Are you going to make the same choice as Pascal? *"Choose life, that you may live"* (Deuteronomy 30:20).

A gift is not a gift unless you accept it. It is your choice. You have the power to accept the covenant. You have the power to reject the covenant. You do not have the power to alter the covenant.

When you enter the covenant, you become aware of God as your heavenly Father. You want to worship Him with a heart of gratitude. The *goyim*, with God's covenant, become the righteous Gentile.

THE RIGHTEOUS GENTILE

*"It is my judgment, therefore, that we should not make it difficult for the Gentiles **who are turning** [emphasis mine] to God"* (Acts 15:19). This verse speaks of the righteous Gentile.

The second type of *goyim* in Scripture is known as the foreigners, in Hebrew: *"Ger Toshev,"* or in Greek: *"Parikia."* They observe the Gentile laws of the Torah, and are given the privilege of becoming a resident alien in the Holy Land. These Gentiles were non-Jews living in Israel, called *"aliens who live among you."*

The word "Hebrew" means "one who has crossed over." Abraham was the first one to be called a Hebrew. When you also take this step, you, like Abraham, become one who has crossed over.

*"Also it was in union with him that **you were circumcised** [emphasis mine] with a circumcision not done by human hands, but accomplished by stripping away the old nature's control over the body."*

*"In this circumcision done by the Messiah, you were buried along with him by **being immersed** [emphasis mine];"*

"and in union with him, you were also raised up along with him by God's faithfulness that worked when he raised Yeshua from the dead. You were dead because of your sins, that is, because of your "foreskin," your old nature."

"But God made you alive along with the Messiah by forgiving you all your sins. He wiped away the bill of charges against us."

*"Because of the regulations, it stood as a testimony against us; but he removed it by nailing it to the **execution-stake** [emphasis mine]. Stripping the rulers and authorities of their power, he made a public spectacle of them, triumphing over them by means of the stake"* (Colossians 2:11-15 CJB).

These verses cannot be used to stop Jews from circumcising their sons. The context will not allow it. This is being applied to Gentiles, not Jews. These verses also cannot be used to teach that the Torah was nailed to the *"execution-stake."*[11] It would be taking the Scriptures out of its context. In fact, the words "law" or "Torah" are never mentioned in the entire letter of Colossians.

What does it mean? There were three processes for a Gentile proselyte to convert to Judaism during the time of Yeshua and Paul. They were circumcision, mikvah (baptism), and a sacrifice. These verses are the only context in Scripture where circumcision, mikvah, and the sacrifice are connected.

Paul wrote these verses to show the Gentile believers they were full members of God's people through trusting God and His Messiah, Yeshua. They have not taken the three physical steps necessary for conversion to non-Messianic Judaism, yet they are considered part of the *"one new man."*

What Is The "Bill Of Charges" Against You?

Anti-torah teachers often interpret these verses as the Messiah nailing the Torah (law) to the execution-stake, but, again, the context of the Scriptures will not allow it. That is not what it says (see appendix 3). It is nailing our sins to the *"execution-stake,"* lining up with Romans 9:30-10:10; Galatians 2:16, 3:23; and Ephesians 2:15.

In Judaism, the relationship between God and man was often described as existing between a debtor and his creditor. A Rabbi once said, *"When a man sins, God writes down the debt of death. If the man repents, the debt is cancelled (declared invalid). If he does not repent, what is recorded remains genuine (valid)"* (Tanhuma Midrash 140b)

During the time of Yeshua, when a convicted man was crucified, the Romans would nail a list of his crimes to the same *"execution-stake."* This type of sign was nailed above Yeshua's head listing his *"crimes"* (John 19:19-22).

The *"certificate of debt consisting of decrees against us"* (Colossians 2:14 ASV) is the "list" of our crimes against God's perfect Torah. They can no longer condemn the believer to death because Yeshua paid the penalty. The "certificate of sin – indebtedness" is the "record book of sin," not the law (Torah) of Moses. The Torah of Moses is not a "book of records."

God's book of sin is recorded in Exodus 32:31-33. After the sin of the Golden Calf, Moses returns to the mountain, and pleads with God with these words:

"And Moses returned unto the LORD, and said, Oh, this people have sinned a great sin, and have made them gods of gold. Yet now, if thou wilt forgive their sin—; and if not, blot me, I pray thee, out of thy book which thou hast written."

"And the LORD said unto Moses, Whosoever hath sinned against me, him will I blot out of my book" (KJV).

During the time of Yeshua and Paul, the normal process to cancel a bond or a debt was by crossing it out with the Greek cross-letter, "chi" (x). The "chi" stood for the phase, "I cross out."

Paul was saying that the *"certificate of debt consisting of decrees"* (Colossians 2:14 ASV) against us, which were being cancelled, was all the debt of sin you owed to Adonai. This was the item nailed to the *"execution-stake."* It was, in a sense, being cancelled with a big "x" on it, as other debts were cancelled in the ancient Greek world. Remember, Yeshua said, "**It** is finished," not "**I am** finished."

According to Scripture, there is higher level of Gentile. By applying this method, the Gentile could become a God fearer.

THE GOD FEARER

"There was a certain man in Caesarea called Cornelius, a centurion of the band called the Italian band."

*"A **devout** [emphasis mine] man, and one that **feared God** [emphasis mine] with all his house, which gave much alms to the people, and prayed to God always"* (Acts 10:1-2 KJV).

The third type of *"goyim"* in Scripture is known as God fearer. He is known in Hebrew as *"Ger Hashair,"* in Greek as *"Eusebes,"* and in English as *"devout."* The Greek word, *"Eusebes"* means "one who is reverent and pious towards God, parents, and others."

The requirements of a *"God fearer,"* according to Jewish custom, were to obey the Gentile commandments of the Torah, including the Sabbath, the dietary and other Jewish instructions according to the Torah, to maintain synagogue discipleship, to worship in the Jewish way of life and to maintain the Jewish customs.

There are many levels of the dietary instructions in the Jewish way of life, but the bottom, base-line foundation could not be violated. The result is the written word of the Torah. Following the instructions of the Torah the Gentile could become...

THE PROSELYTE

The fourth type of "*goyim*" in Scripture is known as the proselyte. In Hebrew, he would be called "*Ger Tzedek*," the "proselyte of righteousness." The word in Hebrew for proselyte is "*proselytes*," meaning, "to come to." The word in Greek is "*proselutos*," meaning, "one who comes from his own people to another." An example of this type of Gentile would be the great-grandmother of David: Ruth.

Another example in scripture would be the Gentile, Caleb, who was one of the twelve spies who went into Canaan. Caleb, whose Hebrew name means, "*dog*," was a leader of the tribe of Judah. Yet, he was a Gentile.

"*Of the tribe of Judah, Caleb the son of Jephunneh*" (Numbers 13:6 ASV).

"*Jephunneh*" is not a Hebrew name. What tribe did his father come from? Scripture gives the answer.

"*Then the children of Judah drew nigh unto Joshua in Gilgal: and **Caleb the son of Jephunneh the Kenizzite** [emphasis mine] said unto him, Thou knowest the thing that Jehovah spake unto Moses the man of God concerning me and concerning thee in Kadesh-barnea*" (Joshua 14:6 ASV).

Where did the Kenizzite tribe come from? Again, look to Scripture:

"*In that day <u>Adonai</u> [my translation] made a covenant with Abram, saying, Unto thy seed have I given this land, from the river of Egypt unto the great river, the river Euphrates: the Kenite, and **the Kenizzite**, and the Kadmonite, and the Hittite, and the Perizzite, and the Rephaim, and the Amorite, and the Canaanite, and the Girgashite, and the Jebusite*" (Genesis 15:18-21 ASV).

Do you have the spirit of Caleb? There are only thirty verses about Caleb, but six times scriptures state that Caleb "*fully followed the Lord*" (Numbers 14:24; 32:12; Deuteronomy 1:36; Joshua 14:8, 9, and14). There were only two people God called His servant, Moses and Caleb. Caleb was called G-d's servant in Numbers 14:24.

"But because my servant Caleb has a different spirit and follows me wholeheartedly, I will bring him into the land he went to, and his descendants will inherit it" (NIV).

When the children of Israel went into the land of Israel to conquer it, they did not drive out the inhabitants as God told them to do. When it came to receiving his inheritance, Caleb took the worst assignment, the land of giants. The three sons of Anak, located in Hebron, were part of the 'Nephilim' and referred to as giants in Deuteronomy 2:10-11.

Caleb did not retire at the age of sixty-five. Twenty years later at the age of eighty-five, he was still fighting and winning battles. He is the only one who succeeded in driving out the inhabitants, as recorded in Joshua 15:13-17. Do you have the spirit of Caleb?

You will need the heart of Ruth and the spirit of Caleb to become a proselyte. You can still have the attributes of Ruth and Caleb, and not make this final step. These attributes are also needed as a God fearer.

These Gentiles at the time of Yeshua had to follow the same requirements as a native-born Jew: all of the God fearer requirements, circumcision, a mikvah, a sacrifice in the temple, and to pay the Temple tax.

There were two classifications of proselytes at the time of Yeshua. One of the classifications was called "righteousness of the Torah." This proselyte used the Torah as a law code. They were motivated by fear, moved to obey God through obligation, and expressed their relationship to God by obedience. Their goal would become isolation. Yeshua spoke about this in Matthew 23:15:

"Woe to you, scribes and Pharisees, hypocrites! For you travel land and sea to win one proselyte, and when he is won, you make him twice as much a son of hell as yourselves" (KJV).

The second classification of proselyte was those Gentiles known as "the keeper of the gate." They saw the Torah as a covenant between them and God.

Instead of obeying God through obligation, they do it because of loyalty. Instead of expressing their relationship to God by obedience, they express it by love. Instead of isolation, their goal was intimacy.

Today, there is a major danger for the Gentile who takes this step. Because there is no temple, there can be no sacrifice. To convert to rabbical Judaism, this step will require three processes: circumcision for the male, the mikvah, and, the last, and most important step: to appear before a "*Bet Din*" to show you understand and accept the obligations of being a religious Jew. This last step will require you to denounce Yeshua as your Messiah and God.

If you are a Gentile and take this last step, you will be issued an *Shtar Giur* ("Certificate of Conversion"), certifying that you are now a Jew. You are not required to take this last step. Your salvation does not depend on it. I am not trying to install fear, but if you make this decision, I feel compelled to give you a warning: I had friends who have taken this last step, and their lives have fallen apart, fulfilling this Scripture:

"Everyone therefore who confesses me before men, him I will also confess before my Father who is in heaven. But whoever denies me before men, him I will also deny before my Father who is in heaven" (Matthew 10:32-33 KJV).

YESHUA, "HATORAH"

Yeshua did not set out to follow the Torah. It was His precise nature to do so. The generation of Jewish believers in Yeshua who existed following the death of the apostles called Yeshua "*HaTorah*," a Hebrew expression that means "*The Torah*."[12] To them, Yeshua was not simply the correct interpretation of the Torah, or the fulfillment of the Tanakh's prophecies. Yeshua was the perfect embodiment of the Torah itself. All that the Torah taught was perfectly lived out in His life (See Appendix 5).

Yeshua's place in history can be found in the words that describe this one solitary life. Allow me to quote it:

"Here is a man who was born in an obscure village, the child of a peasant woman. He grew up in another village. He worked in a carpenter shop until He was thirty. Then for three years, He was an itinerant preacher."

"He never owned a home. He never wrote a book. He never held an office. He never had a family. He never went to college. He never put His foot inside a big city. He never traveled 200 over miles from the place where He was born. He never did one of the things that usually accompany greatness. He had no credentials but Himself…"

"While still a young man, the tide of public opinion turned against Him. His friends ran away. One of them denied Him. He was turned over to His enemies. He went through the mockery of a trial. He was nailed upon a cross between two thieves. While He was dying, His executioners gambled for the only piece of property He had on earth – His coat. When He was dead, He was laid in a borrowed grave through the pity of a friend."

"Nineteen long centuries have come and gone, and today He is the centerpiece of the human race, and leader of the column of progress."

"I am far within the mark when I say that all the armies that ever marched; all of the navies that were ever built; all of the parliaments that ever sat and all the kings that ever reigned, put together, have not effected the life of man upon the earth as powerfully as has that one solitary life."[13]

V   IS YESHUA THE WRITTEN WORD?

*"To one who has faith, no explanation is necessary.
To one without faith, no explanation is possible"*

Thomas Aquinas (1225-1274)

V IS YESHUA THE WRITTEN WORD?

"And the Word became flesh, and dwelt among us (and we beheld his glory, glory as of the only begotten from the Father), full of grace and truth." **(John 1:14 KJV)**

CHANGES IN SCRIPTURE

Yeshua is the firm ladder, but for Yeshua to be your firm ladder, it must have a strong foundation. Without it, the ladder will slip as you climb higher. To create that foundation, the ladder must be placed on the rock, which is the Word of God.

This forces a question: can it be proven that Yeshua is the written Word? Before you can answer this question, you must answer another one. Are the Jewish rabbis more powerful than the Torah itself? The Torah, in Deuteronomy 25:3 (KJV), reads:

"Forty stripes he may give him, he shall not exceed; lest, if he should exceed, and beat him above these with many stripes, then thy brother should seem vile unto thee."

You have read about the forty lashes to be given in case of a serious transgression, yet the ancient sages interpreted the verse to mean giving only thirty-nine. This is not a stand-alone misinterpretation.

There are a number of occasions where the ancient sages reinterpreted the text. They say to wear Tefillin above the hairline, not between the eyes, as the text seems to command. The other phylactery is placed on the arm, not the hand, though strict textual reading would have the Jewish believer to do so.

The Talmud states that the rabbis have more power than the Torah because of this understanding. The Jews also state that nothing is to be added, or diminished from the Talmud. *(Ganz. Tzemach David, par. 1. fol. 34. 1.)*

Are the Jewish rabbis more powerful than the Torah itself? If you believe the Torah, the answer is NO. In Deuteronomy 4:2 it reads:

"In order to obey the mitzvot of ADONAI your God which I am giving you, do not add to what I am saying, and do not subtract from it" (CJB).

God drives His point home by repeating it again:

"Everything I am commanding you, you are to take care to do. Do not add to it, or subtract from it" (Deuteronomy 12:32 CJB).

There is one major difference between the ancient sages and Yeshua. Yeshua is the written Word.

"When Yeshua had finished saying these things, the crowds were amazed at the way he taught, for he was not instructing them like their Torah-teachers but as one who had authority himself" (Matthew 7:28-29 CJB).

Why are these verses important? Believers in Yeshua are instructed to let the Messiah live out His life in them. Your life is to be full of grace, mercy, love, truth, and other godly qualities. This process involves trust in what you were taught.

THE MEANING OF "MEMRA"

"Memra" is an Aramaic word, which is translated as *"word"* in English. The Jewish rabbis used the term, *"Memra"* in the centuries before and after Yeshua when speaking of God's expression of Himself.

The Aramaic Targums, translations of the Hebrew Scriptures into Aramaic during the second Temple Period, speak of a unique individual referred to as *"Memra."* The Targums use the word *"Memra"* to describe a person who is the Creator of the world.

The Jerusalem Targum reads Genesis 1:27 as follows:

"And the Word (Memra) of the Lord created man in His likeness, in the likeness of the Lord, the Lord created, male and female created He them"

Rabbi Tzvi Nassi, a lecturer in Hebrew at Oxford University, writes:

"That this word is the essential and uncreated Word, one of the three Heads, which are One, is evident from His being the Creator of Man, as the Jerusalem paraphrase of Johahan Ben Uziel (Genesis. 1:27) faithfully teaches me... I clearly perceive that the Word is called Adonai, and that through Him (The uncreated, self-existing Word) all things, visible and invisible were created."

To back up his statement, he cites the Jerusalem Targum to Exodus 3:14:

"And the Word (Memra) of the Lord said unto Moses: 'I AM He who said to the World 'BE!' and it was; and in the Future shall say to it 'BE!' and it shall be' and He said: 'Thus thou shall say to the Children of Israel: 'I AM hath sent me to you'" (The Great Mystery, p. 34-35).

The use of the word, *"Memra"* in John's day meant there was a way to express fully the concept of a person who was divine, involved in the creation of the world, and yet able to communicate with and relate to men. John said, *"This 'Memra' (Word) became flesh."* John was asserting that

109

Yeshua not only existed before the world began, but actually did the creating.

In Mark 7:1-13, Yeshua is questioned by a group of Pharisees that may have come from the rabbical school of Shammai. He was asked why His students did not practice the tradition of ritual hand washing. This particular group of Pharisees thought it should be practiced before they had a meal.

The first thing noted about Mark 7:1-13 is that the discussion between Yeshua and the Pharisees were not over the written Torah. It was over the oral Torah. This comes from the phase in 7:3, *"observing the tradition of the elders."* These terms are used to show the difference of the teachings between the oral law, and the commands of the Torah, the written law.

This is a critical point in this whole discussion. If the subject were strictly the written Torah, Yeshua would not have any disagreement with the Pharisees.

Consider another point: Yeshua's problem was not with the oral tradition per se. His problem was with the thinking that it had divine origin and the accompanying divine authority. Yeshua was contending that there were some things in the oral law where some Pharisees were *"neglecting the commandments of God, you were holding to the traditions of men"* (Mark 7:8).

Mark 7:18-23 is a section of Scriptures some anti-Torah teachers use to say Yeshua removed the dietary teachings of Leviticus 11. The key verse to support their position states: *"(Thus He [Yeshua] declared all foods clean)"* (Mark 7:19 ASV). The context does not allow for this interpretation.

There is not a passage in this context where the dietary instructions of Leviticus 11 was a topic of disagreement or brought up in any way.

The phrase *"all foods"* in its context refers to the foods that Yeshua's disciples were eating at the beginning of the chapter. This verse is enclosed in brackets meaning it was not part of the original manuscript. The translator, showing his belief to the meaning of the verse, placed it there. He was wrong. The verse in the brackets cannot be found in some of the biblical translations.

Before you can consider Yeshua did away with the Torah, you must apply these verses to your interpretation:

*"The head cohanim and the whole Sanhedrin looked for some false evidence against Yeshua, so that they might put him to death. **But they didn't find any** [emphasis mine], even though many liars came forward to give testimony"* (Matthew 26:59-60 CJB).

*"The head cohanim and the whole Sanhedrin tried to find evidence against Yeshua, so that they might have him put to death, but **they couldn't find any** [emphasis mine]"* (Mark 14:55 CJB).

Yeshua was, and is, a Torah Observant Jew. If He had taught on changing the Torah, these verses could not exist and be true.

THE SON OF MAN

Faith requires an object to work. The faith object of this ladder is the Son of Man:

"I saw in the night visions, and, behold, one like the Son of man came with the clouds of heaven, and came to the Ancient of days, and they brought him near before him."

"And there was given him dominion, and glory, and a kingdom, that all people, nations, and languages, should serve him: his dominion is an everlasting dominion, which shall not pass away, and his kingdom that which shall not be destroyed" (Daniel 7:13-14 KJV).

Son Of Man vs. The Son Of God

The Title "Son of Man," taken from this verse in Daniel, was used at least forty times by Yeshua, twelve times in the book of John alone. Why did Yeshua favor this title instead of "Son of God," which was more associated with the coming Messiah?

The answer is because "**The** Son of God" was a title, which carried with it the meaning: "King of Israel." This is proven by the fact that Nathaniel placed the two together. It would have been disastrous for Yeshua to allow the people to crown Him "King of Israel."

The "Son of Man" was a title not understood by the common people but understood by the religious leaders. This title was also free from the connection of an earthly kingdom of Israel.

The Pharisees tried to get Yeshua crucified for sedition, but Yeshua completely thwarted them. They finally had to admit to Pilate that they wanted Yeshua dead because He claimed to be the "Son of God."

"The Jews answered him, You have a law, and by your law he ought to die, because he made himself the Son of God" (John 19:7 KJV).

The Pharisees knew that the "Son of Man" was the title of the Messiah as the "Son of God," but they were trying to trick Yeshua into using the "Son of God" title. At the climax of His trial, Caiaphas placed Yeshua under oath, and Yeshua used the other term, as recorded in the Gospel of Matthew.

*"But <u>Yeshua</u> [my translation] held his peace. And the high priest answered and said unto him, I adjure thee by the living God, that thou tell us whether thou be the <u>Messiah</u> [my translation], **the Son of God** [emphasis mine]. <u>Yeshua</u> [my translation] saith unto him, Thou hast said: nevertheless I say unto you, Hereafter shall ye see the **Son of man** [emphasis mine] sitting on the right hand of power, and coming in the clouds of heaven"* (Matthew 26:63-64 KJV).

As said before, the Sanhedrin accepted the term "Son of Man" as equal to "Son of God," and certified it to Pilate. Again, look at the Scriptures recorded by John:

"The Jews answered him, we have a law, and by our law he ought to die, because he made himself the Son of God" (John 19:7 KJV).

Yeshua preferred the "Son of Man" to other titles. It was free from any possible misrepresentations.

Emil Von Ludwig's Book – The Problem

Emil Von Ludwig's book "The Son of Man," published in 1962, made this title the grounds of his thesis that Yeshua never claimed to be anything but a man. This is the book where the anti-missionaries for "Jews for Judaism" get their information concerning the title "Son of Man," and they use the author's arguments.

The arguments have a major flaw. This thesis is contradicted and disproved by the best of all the judges at that time: the Sanhedrin itself. They accepted the title, and certified it to the governor as being equivalent in every way to "**the** Son of God."

Also Yeshua's own use of the title "Son of Man" leaves no doubt as to its being connected to deity and the Godhead. Did Yeshua use it in such a manner as to diminish His claim of divinity?

No. Yeshua, by using the title "Son of Man," meant to affirm His deity and Godhead just as the title "Son of God" could have done it.

However, the title "Son of Man" added the advantage of stressing His unique relationship with the human race as well.

"**The** Son of Man," as backed up by Scripture, cannot be any mortal being. The original Greek words cannot mean "**A** Son of Man," but "**The** Son of Man."

Within the context of the conversation with Nathaniel, Yeshua used the title "Son of Man" in exactly the same way the title "Son of God" was understood. Yeshua also used this title in connection with His power to forgive sins (Matthew

9:6), in His Lordship over the Sabbath (Matthew 12:8), in His second coming in glory (Matthew 19:28), in His resurrection (Matthew 17:23), in His seeking and saving the lost (Luke 19:10), and in His coming back in the final judgment (Matthew 26:64).

DIVORCE AND REMARRIAGE – PART 1

The Torah Parsha of "KiTaitzei" (Deuteronomy 21:10 – 25:19) deals with an array of commandments, many dealing between man and his fellow man. They range from issues concerning lost objects and the responsibilities of Jews to care for their neighbor's misplaced items to fulfilling pledges and lending money. They also deal with the conduct with war between nations and war in your living room.

Of the seventy-four divine commands recorded in this Torah section, one of the hardest to teach and most misunderstood is the teaching about divorce and remarriage. If Yeshua were to speak publicly today about divorce, He would be lambasted as being harsh, judgmental, politically incorrect, and unbending. He would be silenced because His words would be too painful to a hurting generation that has suffered so much pain from divorce.

Not only is there disagreement about this matter, but also it is exceptionally powerful disagreement. The love that exists between a man and his wife is the continuous symbol used in Solomon's Song of Songs to declare the unshakable love God has for His nation. There is one problem: divorce is also a fact of life. This Parsha discusses the method of divorce. It also tells us why marriages last and end.

"When a man takes a wife, and marries her, and it happens that she find no favor in his eyes, because he has found some indecency ["ervah"] in her, that he shall write her a bill of divorce, and give it in her hand, and send her out of his house. When she is departed out of his house, she may go and be another man's [wife]. If the latter husband hate

her, and write her a bill of divorce, and give it in her hand, and send her out of his house; or if the latter husband die, who took her to be his wife; her former husband, who sent her away, may not take her again to be his wife, after that she is defiled; for that is abomination before the LORD: and you shall not cause the land to sin, which the LORD your God gives you for an inheritance.

When a man takes a new wife, he shall not go out in the army, neither shall he be charged with any business: he shall be free at home one year, and shall cheer his wife whom he has taken" (Deuteronomy 24:1-5 KJV).

In verse 5, the words, "cheer (*saw-makh*) his wife" did not just mean to tell jokes! It allowed the couple to become fully grounded, and diminished or removed occasions for the divorces.

Rabbi Shammai, known for a strict judgment in most matters, said divorce should only occur over a matter of immorality. Rabbi Hillel, who died shortly before Yeshua began his public ministry, said that divorce is permitted *"even if she burns his soup."* Rabbi Akiva, who lived a generation or two after Yeshua, and whose devotion and gratitude to his wife was legendary, said, *"even if he finds a nicer woman, he may divorce."*

Also consider this: Assyrian and Hittite law gives the · husband the right to kill both guilty parties on the spot if caught in the act, but the executioner in Israel was always the community, the state, or its representatives.

What does this mean? Adultery must be seen as a crime that threatened society, not simply as an act against the husband. These two factors in the Torah—the role of the state in prosecution, and the death penalty given to the guilty parties—point to criminal rather than civil law.

The first thing noticed concerning the teaching of divorce and remarriage in Deuteronomy is that the context of the laws seem to be that of protecting the second marriage, rather than dealing directly about divorce itself. It looks as if these laws were intended to preserve the second marriage. Once the divorcee has entered a second marriage, there is no possibility of the first husband reclaiming her. Reunion is forbidden and the second marriage is guaranteed.

If this is correct, the Torah brings out two things. Divorce is permissible under some circumstances, and remarriage is permissible under certain circumstances. According to the Torah, the one condition for divorcing a wife appears to be if the husband finds some unchaste thing in her. The Hebrew word in Deuteronomy 24:1 is broader than just adultery. In fact, if adultery were the problem, the solution was not divorce, but stoning.

The Greek word for unchastity, like its Hebrew counterpart in Deuteronomy 24:1, is much more extensive then merely adultery. The Hebrew word, "*ervah*," means "nakedness, nudity, (implying shameful exposure)." The Greek word for unchastity, "*porneia*," has two meanings: "illicit sexual intercourse," and "the worship of idols."

A number of scholars believe this is part of the betrothal period because of this understanding. The betrothal in ancient Israel was considered as legally binding as marriage itself. In fact, the partners were sometimes called husband and wife. The only differences were the couple did not live with each other and had no sexual relationship with each other.

Unchastity found in the wife would be when the marriage was finally consummated the husband found out she was not a virgin but was unfaithful to him before or during the engagement or betrothal period. It is then that he had a legal right to divorce her. Not only does this line up with the Torah text, but also it best explains Yeshua's teaching on the subject.

There are two things connected with the Word of God and the God who gave that revelation. First, all Yeshua spoke was absolute truth, and second, all He did was an expression of His actual nature: grace.

Consider how Yeshua taught on the subject of divorce and remarriage. Yeshua taught about this topic in two main passages. The first passage is found in Matthew 5:31-32;

"It was also said, 'Whoever shall put away his wife, let him give her a writing of divorce, but I tell you that whoever puts away his wife, except for the cause of sexual immorality, makes her an adulteress; and whoever marries her when she is put away commits adultery" (Matthew 5:31-32 KJV).

Here, it looks like Yeshua was correcting some misguided Torah teaching that permitted divorce for any reason. Yeshua expresses this erroneous view in verse 31 as being based on a misquotation of Deuteronomy 24:1. The mistaken Torah teachers were leaving absent in their teachings the phrase that says, *"for he has found in her a matter of immorality."* By leaving out this phase, these teachers taught a liberal view of divorce and remarriage.

This leaves us with two observations: that the Jewish rabbis are not more powerful than the Torah, and that Yeshua is the written Word.

DIVORCE AND REMARRIAGE – PART 2

The second major divorce and remarriage passage is found in Matthew 19:3-9.

"And there came unto him Pharisees, trying him, and saying, Is it lawful for a man to put away his wife for every cause? And he answered and said, Have ye not read, that he who made them from the beginning made them male and female, and said, For this cause shall a man leave his father and mother, and shall cleave to his wife; and the two shall become one flesh? so that they are no more two, but one flesh. What therefore God hath joined together, let not man put asunder."

"They say unto him, Why then did Moses command to give a bill of divorcement, and to put her away? He said unto them, Moses for your hardness of heart suffered you to put

away your wives: but from the beginning, it hath not been so. And I say unto you, Whosoever shall put away his wife, except for unchastity, and shall marry another, commits adultery: and he that marries her when she is put away commits adultery" (KJV).

These verses give a more extensive treatment of the subject by Yeshua. Yeshua, on the one hand, restates what both He and the Torah in Deuteronomy 24 have already said. Again, the use of the word, "unchastity" in verse 9 is the exception clause.

This is also perfectly compatible with the Torah. If the betrothal view is correct, a husband may legally divorce his new wife if he finds she was unfaithful to him before or during the betrothal period.

Yeshua, on the other hand, adds another thought, which has never been stated. He tells us two things. The Torah of Moses regulated life in the redeemed community, which lived in a sin-foundational world. As a result, things like unchastity before marriage had to be treated fairly. Second, God's ideal of marriage is the type existing before the fall in the Garden of Eden. Yeshua, although willing to let the Torah regulation to be practiced, also encouraged His followers to conduct their marriages as if they were in the Garden of Eden.

This understanding produces five observations. First, nowhere in Scripture does it command that a divorce must take place. This leads to the second point, the one Yeshua is making in Matthew 19. As new creations, it is possible to conduct your marriage as if you are back in the Garden of Eden before the fall. If you find adultery or unfaithfulness, either before or after marriage, it is possible to forgive.

Third, it took a *"bill of divorcement,"* known as a *"get"* to dissolve a betrothal relationship legally. A husband could not send his wife away casually. He had to *sleep on it* and go to court to end it. He would also be deprived of his wife's dowry. This process made divorce too expensive for most husbands.

Fourth, both were free to pursue other possible relationships. And fifth, Yeshua taught, and supported the Torah when he discussed marriage. Even when He said Moses gave permission for a divorce "because of the hardness of your hearts," it was not in opposition of the Torah but in agreement with it.

WHAT DID BARABBAS KNOW?

To accept Yeshua as the Word is to believe in Him. The Scripture, according to the apostle John, states that life begins with looking to the "Son of Man."

"Just as Moshe lifted up the serpent in the desert, so must the Son of Man be lifted up; so that everyone who trusts in him may have eternal life" (John 3:14-15 CJB).

Before Moses lifted up the brazen serpent, people died. When Moses lifted up the brazen serpent, (Numbers 21:4-9), people lived. The children of Israel had to know three things to prevent dying. They needed to know they were bitten, that there was a God given remedy against death, and that the remedy was not good until applied.

These same three processes must be applied to Yeshua for you to have eternal life. You must know that you have been bitten by sin, that God has provided a remedy against eternal death, and that the remedy must be applied to receive God's healing. The remedy comes from the ladder, Yeshua.

There is one man in Scripture that understood this substitution process: Barabbas. He knew he was a justly condemned sinner. He knew Yeshua was an innocent sufferer. He knew the innocent sufferer has taken his place. He knew he had done nothing to merit that substitution. He also knew that Yeshua's substitution in his place satisfied the law. Do you have the same knowledge as Barabbas?

"And I, if I be lifted up from the earth, will draw all men unto me" (John 12:32 KJV).

YESHUA AND THE SCRIPTURES

When you examine the Scriptures, you can find Yeshua in all sixty-six books. Consider this:

In Genesis He is our Creator. In Exodus He is our deliverer. In Leviticus, He is our eternal sacrifice. In Numbers, He is our trusted guide. In Deuteronomy, He is our redeeming prophet. In Joshua, He is our divine captain of the Lord's hosts. In Judges, He is our steadfast God. In Ruth, He is our kinsman redeemer. In 1 Samuel, He is our interceding king. In 2 Samuel, He is our anointed king. In 1 Kings, He is our wise king. In 2 Kings, He is our reigning king.

In 1 Chronicles, He is our sovereign God. In 2 Chronicles, He is the glory of the Lord. In Ezra, He is the fulfillment of God's promise. In Nehemiah, He is the re-builder of lives. In Esther, He is the hidden teacher. In Job, He is our faith in the fullness of God.

In Psalms, He is our song of praise. In Proverbs, He is our wisdom. In Ecclesiastes, He is our only hope. In The Song of Solomon, He is our bridegroom. In Isaiah, He is our Messiah. In Jeremiah, He is our compassionate friend. In Lamentations, He is our passion in the Lord. In Ezekiel, He is our watchman. In Daniel, He is our rescuer in time of need. In Hosea, He is our faithful husband. In Joel, He is our outpouring of God's goodness.

In Amos, He is our burden bearer. In Obadiah, He is our highest authority. In Jonah, He is the width of God's mercy. In Micah, He is our coming Messiah. In Nahum, He is our avenger. In Habakkuk, He is the foundation of our faith. In Zephaniah, He is the glory of Israel. In Haggai, He is our restorer. In Zechariah, He is our Prince of Peace. In Malachi, He is our glorious promise.

In Matthew, He is the King of the Jews. In Mark, He is the Son of God. In Luke, He is the Son of Man. In John, He is the Word made flesh. In Acts, He is the power on high, the wind and the fire of the *Ruach Hakodesh*. In Romans, He is our salvation. In 1 Corinthians, He is our believing ideal. In 2 Corinthians, He is seen as our victory over all things.

In Galatians, He is our liberator. In Ephesians, He is the chief cornerstone. In Philippians, He is the supplier of our needs. In Colossians, He is the fullness of the Godhead. In 1 Thessalonians, He is our soon and coming King. In 2 Thessalonians, He is the mighty returning Messiah. In 1 Timothy, He is our mediator. In 2 Timothy, He is our faithful witness. In Titus, He is our blessed hope.

In Philemon, He is our brother and friend. In Hebrews, He is our High Priest. In James, He is the source of all blessings. In 1 Peter, He is our chief Shepherd. In 2 Peter, He is our Savior. In 1, 2, and 3 John, He is our righteousness, love, and truth. In Jude, He is our glory, majesty, and power. And in Revelation, He is the First and the Last, the Lord God Almighty. Yeshua is the Living Word!

To prevent a person from *"reading someone else's mail,"* accurate meanings must be applied to individual verses. This can be determined, as a rule, by the scripture's context. The steps moving one type of Gentile to a different type are called biblical faith. This forces the question, what is *"biblical faith?"*

VI   THE LEAP OF FAITH

"A man with God is always in the majority"

John Knox (c1513 – 1572)

VI.   THE LEAP OF FAITH

—◆◆◆—

> *"Come Now, and let us REASON TOGETHER,"* saith
> the Lord: *"Though your sins be as Scarlet, they SHALL*
> *BE as white as snow; though they be red like crimson,*
> *they shall be as wool"* **(Isaiah 1:18 ASV)**

DOES "BLIND FAITH" EXIST?

A.W. Tozer said, *"Without faith it is impossible to please God, but not all 'faith' pleases God. Faith in faith is faith astray. To hope for heaven by means of such faith is to drive in the dark across a deep chasm on a bridge that does not quite reach the other side."*

What does *"the **evidence** [emphasis mine] of things not seen,"* as recorded in Hebrews 11:1, mean? This verse tells you there is no blind leap. Faith is greatly misunderstood by most people, being presented as what a person relies when all reason is against him.

Faith can go beyond reason, but it will never go against it. Faith is neither believing what you want in the face of evidence to the contrary, nor the power of believing what you know is untrue. That is religious wishful thinking, squeezing out spiritual hope by intense acts of sheer will.

125

The first episode of the movie Star Wars had a much-quoted line, "May the force be with you." Some people believe faith is a force or power that comes from within you. Once emotional passion enters, human reason, without God's grace, has as much chance of retaining truth as a snowflake has of retaining its shape in the mouth of a blast furnace.

A large number of people believe faith is a force within itself. The electronic church teaches that if you have enough *"faith-force,"* you can accomplish anything. There is a problem with this interpretation.

These words have been said before, but they bear repeating: *"Faith is embedded in trust."* Faith is not a force. It is entrenched in trust. Faith allows dependence, or trust, on someone else when you cannot help yourself. Trust allows you to go to the Source of the power; but trust is not the power. Understanding this, how do you act in response to the argument: can you have faith in something you know is true?

The dispute goes like this: if you know it to be true, than no faith can be involved. Lack of knowledge explains the meaning of the leap of faith, but it reduces the believer's conviction to wishful thinking. Conviction is the fruit of hope.

"Don't ask questions, just have faith," or "Make it happen, just believe." Is this category of faith different from wishing? What makes the believer's wishing unlike the Hindu or an atheist, if not based on facts and evidence? Nothing!

Nowhere in Scripture does it show where the blind leap of faith exists. The blind leap of faith is never what God had in mind. The *Ruach Hakodesh* does not work in a blind, ungrounded faith in the heart. You believe because of, not in spite of, the evidence.

In the new birth, the *Ruach Hakodesh* (Holy Spirit) does not make a man a believer regardless of the evidence. His purpose is to clear away the smog from a man's eyes to enable him to accept the belief based on the evidence. Consider using the word "trust" instead of "faith." It better reflects the meaning of scripture when called to believe. Biblical faith is persuasion connected with your past experience. Trust is dependence applied to your present as well as your future.

Simple faith and biblical trust are two different things. They both have two different Hebrew and Greek words. Faith, which in Hebrew is *"emuwnah"* and in Greek is *"pistis,"* means a conviction based upon hearing. Trust, which in Hebrew is *"bitachon"* and in Greek is *"peithe,"* means to have confidence, dependence, and security, and to be established.

Here is an example. You may have the faith to get married, but you don't work out trust in marriage until you say the words, "I do." Faith is not wishing. Faith's conviction has a confidence because it is tied to trust.

There is no discrepancy between knowing something is true, called "evidence," and having faith in it. This statement forces the question: where do you place your trust? Again, Scripture gives you the answer:

*"But these which have been recorded are here so that you may **trust** [emphasis mine] that Yeshua is the Messiah, the Son of God, and that by this **trust** [emphasis mine] you may have life because of who He is"* (John 20:31 CJB).

"Therefore, let the whole house of Israel know beyond doubt that God has made Him both Lord and Messiah this Yeshua, whom you executed on a stake" (Acts 2:36 CJB).

Do you know Yeshua is the Son of God by hope, or by trust and faith, attached with evidence?

*"And declared to be the Son of God with **power** [emphasis mine], according to the spirit of holiness, by the resurrection from the dead"* (Romans 1:4 KJV).

Trust produces an act of faith, which is grounded by being persuaded of the truth because of the evidence. You know Yeshua is the Son of God because He was raised from the dead; that is evidence. Trust, faith and reason joined hands when Yeshua used objective evidence to legalize His claims (Mark 2:5-12; John 2:18-21; John 10:30-33, 37-38; John 15:24-25; John 20:24-29).

Trust and faith bridges the space between the unknown "'X' percent" probability, and the evidence of certainty. Here are some examples: crossing the street, starting your car, driving today (that is called risky faith), and sitting on a chair; all these examples are exercises of faith, produced by your past experiences of trust. Since you do not have any assurance about anything, sacred or secular, then it is trust, through faith, that allows you to commit.

In a court of law, a judge tells the jury to decide, based on the probability of the evidence presented, the guilt or innocence. The evidence will never be a hundred percent conclusive. A juror who witnessed the crime, which would be a hundred percent, would not be part of the jury. If decisions were delayed until hundred percent certainties existed, every trial would be a mistrial. Decisions are based on trust, backed by the faith in the evidence.

The atheist maintains the universe is a gigantic accident with no purpose, yet they must live as if their life and relationships have meaning. He exercises faith daily. The atheist's blind faith is against overwhelming evidence and sound reason; the atheist's faith says, "God does not exist."

His blind leap of faith gives the atheist more blind faith than the believer. The atheist has blind faith, but does not have saving faith. What is saving faith?

THREE ELEMENTS OF SAVING FAITH

Saving faith is composed of three fundamentals. The first element, as recorded in Romans 10:14-17, is called data, evidence, or knowledge.

"But how can they call on someone if they haven't trusted in him? And how can they trust in someone if they haven't heard about him? And how can they hear about someone if no one is proclaiming him? And how can people proclaim him unless God sends them? - as the Tanakh puts it, 'How beautiful are the feet of those announcing good news about good things!'"

"The problem is that they haven't all paid attention to the Good News and obeyed it. For Yesha'yahu says, 'ADONAI, who has trusted what he has heard from us?' So trust comes from what is heard, and what is heard comes through a word proclaimed about the Messiah" (CJB).

This is an act of the senses. Knowledge, left alone, is not saving faith.

The second element in saving faith is the acknowledgement of data that is classified as true. This is an act of the intellect.

"For unto us was the gospel preached, as well as unto them: but the word preached did not profit them, not being mixed with faith in them that heard it. For we which have believed do enter into rest, as he said, As I have sworn in my wrath, if they shall enter into my rest: although the works were finished from the foundation of the world. For he spake in a certain place of the seventh day on this wise, And God did rest the seventh day from all his works" (Hebrews 4:2-4 KJV).

These two fundamentals together are called historical faith. It is not saving faith. The Scripture says, *"You believe that God is one, you do well; the demons also believe, and shudder"* (James 2:19 ASV). These two essentials are necessary preconditions for saving faith. An example would be the prerequisites required before receiving a degree. Other classes are still mandatory.

The third component in saving faith is the trust in the knowledge you received. This becomes an act of the will. It involves self-surrender, commitment, and reliance. This can only be done by commitment and trust in Yeshua as your Savior through the *Ruach Hakodesh*. This process produces grace. This can be understood through James 4:6, using the Amplified Bible.

*"But He gives more and more grace (power of the Roach Hakodesh to meet the evil tendency and all others fully). That is why He says, 'God sets Himself against the proud and haughty, but gives **grace** [emphasis mine] (continually) to the lowly – those who are humble-minded (enough to receive it)"* (AMP).

The grace of God must be present before the will of God can be in your life. If all three fundamentals are not present, you do not –cannot- possess saving faith. Any other belief is counterfeit, and therefore unbelief. Even the most genuine, but misplaced, faith or trust leads to ruin. *"There is a way which seems right to a man, but its end is the way of death"* (Proverbs 14:12 ASV).

On Wednesday, April 10, 1912, shortly before noon, the largest ship in the world at that time, the *Titanic*, began her maiden voyage to New York from South Hampton, England with two thousand, two hundred twenty-three passengers and crewmembers aboard.

Everything went well until Sunday morning, April 14, when a wireless message came to the ship from a steamer named *Corinia*. The message told about other steamers reporting icebergs and where they saw them.

After lunch another steamer, the *Californian*, called the *Titanic* by wireless to tell her about three icebergs. The operator of the *Titanic* was figuring his accounts and did not bother to copy the message.

Not long afterward, the *Baltic*, another ship, called to tell about the icebergs in the way. The operator took the message and sent it to the captain. Six hours later, the captain had the message posted on the bulletin board for the officers to read.

In spite of these warnings, no one on the Titanic paid any attention to them. Everybody thought that she was such a good ship that nothing could sink her.

Not long before midnight, the wireless operator on the *Californian* called the operator on the *Titanic* to tell him that they were surrounded by ice. The first time he had called, the *Titanic's* operator paid no attention to him. This time the operator told him to keep quiet!

At eleven-forty, a lookout shouted, "iceberg." Then the officer on the bridge signaled the engine room to stop the engines; then to reverse the engines, but it was too late. At the speed of twenty knots per hour, it struck an iceberg whose jagged points below the water pierced the plating on the starboard side and a great hole over three hundred feet long had been cut into the ship.

At twelve-thirty came the orders: "All passengers on deck with life belts on." At two-thirty, as the hands on the deck played, "Nearer, My God, to Thee," the *Titanic* sank and one thousand five hundred seventeen passengers and crewmembers went to a watery grave.[14]

They died because the operator's trust was misguided. His misplaced faith was wrong because the object of his trust was wrong. He was among the many people who believed that the *Titanic* was unsinkable.

Here is another example:

Years ago, a corps of civil engineers came to Johnstown, Pennsylvania, and went up into the mountains to examine the dam which controlled the waters of the stream which flowed down into the valley. They came back to the town and said to the people, "The dam is unsafe. The people in the valley are in constant danger." The people said to them, "You can't scare us."

That fall, the engineers came back and examined the dam again and said to the people in the valley, "We warn you people again; you are in danger every hour." They laughed at them again; and said, "Scare us if you can." The engineers went up again in the spring and warned the people once more, but the people said, "We have been hearing that so many times. Scare us if you can."

About fifteen days later, a boy came down into the valley riding on a horse at full speed shouting, "Run for your lives! The dam has gone and the water is coming!" The people only laughed at him, but he did not wait to hear their laughter. He went down the mountain still shouting the warning.

In a very few minutes, the dirty water came rushing down and in less than thirty minutes after the water struck the town, Johnstown was in ruins and more than three thousand seven hundred of those who lived in the town were standing in the presence of God.[15]

Their misguided trust was in the dam, not the words of the engineers. They paid the highest price for that mistrust.

Additional examples in our time consist of the Heaven's Gate and the Jim Jones groups. When warnings are given, you still have free choice. When faced with this type of decision, let this Scripture be your deciding factor:

"He heard the sound of the trumpet, and took not warning; his blood shall be upon him. But he that taketh warning shall deliver his soul" (Ezekiel 33:5 KJV).

Does that mean you can argue or reason people into the kingdom of God? No – you are told in scripture that a person can believe if, and when, God calls and enable them through the work of the *Ruach Hakodesh* (John 1:13; 6:44, 65; Romans 9:16; Ephesians 2:8-10; 1 Corinthians 2:14).

The actual ability to hear, consider, and respond to the message of the *Brit Hadashah* is, from the first to the last, the gift of God (Romans 1:17; Ephesians 2:8-10). However, the *Ruach Hakodesh* does not operate independently of the three essentials of knowledge, evidence, and solid reason(s) (Acts 17:22,34; 1 Peter 3:15; Acts 27:22-26, 29-34).

THE GREATEST COMMANDMENT

After a discussion on the resurrection, a Torah Teacher asked Yeshua a question. He said, *"Which is the most important mitzvah [commandment] of them all?"* Consider Yeshua's answer:

"Yeshua answered, 'The most important is 'Shema Yisra'el, Adonai Eloheinu, Adonai Echad' [Hear, O Israel, the Lord our God, the Lord is one] and you are to love Adonai your God with all your heart, with all your soul, with all your understanding [mind] and with all your strength. The second is this: 'You are to love your neighbor as yourself'. There is no other mitzvah greater than these" (Mark 12:29-31 CJB).

Without a love affair with God, you lack the motivation and passion to do His work. How is that love relationship to be worked out? Yeshua gave us four ways:

"With All Your Heart"

To love the Lord with all your heart means to love Him with pure devotion. When you love someone with all your heart, you think about him or her almost all the time. It becomes the priority in your life, and you call this being in love. It means your heart is devoted to him or her, and you are faithful to him or her. The Scripture calls it your first love.

When you meet Yeshua for the first time, the excitement of getting to know Him consumes you. It becomes a passion in your life, which moves you to the second way for the love relationship to be worked out.

"With All Your Soul"

The soul speaks of your emotions. This means that your love for God should be full of passion. When you think of a love affair, you think of passion: a hot-hearted, passionate, consuming love.

Here is the problem: our culture has made people disillusioned and they have become apathetic. The word *"apathetic"* literally means "without passion." In the Song of Solomon, the passionate love you have for God can be compared to that between a man and a woman. What does this mean? Real love is passionate love. Your love for Yeshua begins with pure devotion, than expresses itself by being full of passion, but there is another building block.

"With All Your Mind"

This process is a love that is thoroughly considered. There is a biblical teaching, which contends that the mind can get into the way of your relationship with God. It is true that God cannot be figured out by human minds, but if you wait until you have the process a hundred percent figured out, you might not get in on the blessing in the process.

It is apparent from scripture that God fully intends for your mind to be involved in your love for him. You are told that your mind is to be renewed. A mind committed to the Messiah and being transformed by His renewing power can be a tremendous benefit to the kingdom.

A mind committed to God will become a mind into which God will pour His wisdom and knowledge. It is said you only use about ten percent of your brain. Maybe God is the one who must activate the other ninety percent.

"With All Your Strength"

Your love involves action and must be lived out. To love God with all your strength means to love God in all that you do. Ecclesiastes 9:10 reads, *"Whatever task comes your way to do, do it with all your strength; because in Sh'ol, where you will go, there is neither working nor planning, neither knowledge nor wisdom"* (CJB).

If your love is in the heart only, you have sentimentalism. If your love is in the head only, you have intellectualism. To be alive, the love for God must be lived out in the lives of those who believe. Otherwise, it doesn't make any distinction at all. James says that you should be "*doers of the word*" (James 1:22 KJV).

Yeshua was explaining the two most important concepts in life. The first concept is to have your theology accurate to whom God is, and the second is to respond to Him by loving Him with an affection characterized by keeping His commandments.

Yeshua added one item to the Shama: love with your mind. Why? Your mind is where you receive a mental picture of your future. Without the Word of God, it will be grounded on experience. There is a war for your faith, and to win, you must fight. Where is the battlefield for your faith fought?

THE FOUR BATTLEFIELDS OF FAITH

The lady in the passenger seat happens to look up just as they pass through an intersection and sees that the light was red.

She says nothing. A few minutes later, they approach another intersection. Again, the car cruises right through the red light.

At this point, she turns to the driver and says, "Hazel, you need to drive more carefully or you are going to get us killed. You just went through two red lights."

Hazel turns with a surprised look on her face and says, "Oh, am I driving?"

Sometimes it seems as if many believers are following the same course. They blindly drive down one road after another, without a clue where they are going or where they have been.

Albert Einstein said, "*Insanity: doing the same thing over and over again, and expecting different results.*" [16]

Are you still following the same paths that lead to nowhere? Exactly who's driving anyway? If it is you at the wheel, maybe it is time to try something new.

You are in the fight to the death to lay hold of eternal life, whether you want to fight or not. This warfare is over what you believe.

To win, you must know where the battlegrounds of your faith are fought and why you must fight. The struggle for your faith is in your mind, and will be fought on four battlefield fronts. What are the four battlefields of faith?

Battlefield 1 – What You Hear

Your first battlefield to be won is **what you hear.** The Scriptures say, "*So then faith cometh by hearing, and hearing by the word of God*" (Romans 10:17 KJV).

The struggle for your faith and soul begins on this front line battleground. Faith, which operates from your experience of trust, must be fed to put down roots.

This involves continually hearing the Word of God. When you hear the Word of God, your passion increases, hope comes, and through hope, faith. This is needed to eliminate doubt. James 1:6-7 says the wavering man will receive nothing.

Battlefield 2 – What You Think

Your second battlefield is **what you think**. "*Now faith is the substance of things hoped for, the evidence of things not seen*" (Hebrews 11:1 KJV). You need a clear vision for your life. Faith must have substance. Your vision is the blueprint, or substance, of your faith. What provides the blueprint?

"*And do not be conformed to this world, but be transformed by the renewing of your mind that you may prove what the will of God is, that which is good, acceptable and perfect*" (Romans 12:2 KJV).

You must control your mental process, or you will pay with the loss of the power of God on your life. This can be accomplished by applying the blood of Yeshua to your mind. This control becomes an ongoing process of the consecration of your will to the will of God.

"...Whatever is true, whatever is honorable, whatever is right, whatever is pure, whatever is lovely, whatever is of good repute, if there is any excellence and if anything worthy of praise, dwell on these things" (Philippians. 4:8 ASV).

Battlefield 3 – What You Say

Your third battlefield deals with **what you say.** The Scriptures say, *"By faith we understand that the worlds were prepared by the word of God so that what is seen was not made out of things which are visible"* (Hebrews 11:3 KJV). Everything you see has a spiritual root. You must have a plan on what you say. God framed the world by the words He spoke.

The Word of God is also the container of your faith. You must put the Word of God in your mouth. Out of the abundance of the heart, the mouth, through the power of the *Ruach Hakodesh*, speaks. The words you speak today frame the vision you have for tomorrow, but you must not speak those words in fear. If spoken in fear, Satan wins.

Once these three battlefields have been fought and won, you have applied the three agents of sanctification on your life: The word of God, which is what you hear, increasing your passion. The blood, which is what you think, giving you a vision. And third, the *Ruach Hakodesh*, which is what you say, applying your plan. From this advantage, you have the authority to put your body under subjection, which is the fourth battlefield.

Battlefield 4 – What You Do

Your fourth and final battlefield is **what you do** *"Even so faith if it has no works, is dead being by itself"* (James 2:17 KJV). You will not win the war if you win the first three battlefields and decide not to fight the fourth.

Winning the fourth battlefield equals total sanctification. You believe the scriptures or you don't - your choice; but you will take action on what you believe. Satan does not want your life. He wants your faith! If you lose your faith, you lose your trust. When Satan has your faith, he has your life. Have you not read these words?

"Do you not know that when you present yourselves to someone as slaves for obedience, you are slaves of the one whom you obey, either of sin resulting in death, or of obedience resulting in righteousness" (Romans 6:16 ASV).

HOW TO DEAL WITH SCRIPTURE CONTRADICTIONS

Every believer with a theological point of view thinks his view is scriptural. Picking a verse that seems to support your view may result in one Scripture text being placed against another, creating a contradiction. How do you solve this problem?

Keep one goal in mind. Your question should be, "What does the *Bible* teach?" not, "What does the *verse* seem to teach?" The goal forces the question, "How do you learn what the Scriptures teach?"

You learn by choosing an interpretation that makes sense of all appropriate verses. You must determine if the verses being cited speak in one voice, or has more than one possible meaning. If the verses speak in one voice, even after looking at the text from different angles, it is hard to visualize any other meaning. If the proof texts have more than one meaning, choosing one of the alternate meanings could remove the obvious contradiction. Let's look at two examples.

What Order?

Our first example considers the repentance, *T'zilah*, and salvation issue by asking two questions: What is the order?

Is *T'zilah* (water baptism) necessary for salvation, or is it a proper act of obedience *after* a person becomes a believer?

When you look at case one, the order would be faith, than the *T'zilah*, resulting in salvation, but if you look at case two, the order would be faith, resulting in salvation, followed by the *T'zilah*. Let's look at case one.

"And Kefa [Peter] answered them, 'Turn from sin, return to God, and each of you be immersed on the authority of Yeshua, the Messiah into forgiveness of your sins, and you will receive the gift of the Ruach Hakodesh!'" (Acts 2:38 CJB).

When you look at these scriptures, it seems to say that if the penitent believers will undergo the water baptism *"for [emphasis mine] the forgiveness of sins,"* then repentance and belief are not enough. The order appears to be faith, then the water baptism, resulting in salvation.

That could have no problem, but now let us look at case two.

"Kefa [Peter] was still saying these things when the Ruach Hakodesh fell on all who were hearing the message All the believers from the Circumcision faction who had accompanied Kefa [Peter] were amazed that the gift of the Ruach Hakodesh was also being poured out on the goyim, for they heard them speaking in tongues and praising God."

*"Kefa's response was, 'Is anyone prepared to prohibit these people from being immersed in water? After all, they have received the Ruach Hakodesh, **just as we did** [emphasis mine].' And he ordered that they be immersed in the name of Yeshua the Messiah. Then they asked Kefa to stay on with them for a few days"* (Acts 10:44-48 CJB).

This is undeniable evidence to Peter that these Gentiles have "received the *Ruach Hakodesh* just as [he] did."

Other verses make it clear that possessing the *Ruach Hakodesh* is **proof** of salvation. Here are two examples:

"Furthermore, you who heard the message of the truth, the Good News offering you deliverance, and put your trust in the Messiah were **sealed by Him** *[emphasis mine] with the promised Ruach Hakodesh, who guarantees our inheritance until we come into possession of it and thus bring Him praise commensurate with His glory"* (Ephesians 1:13-14 CJB).

"But you, you do not identify with your old nature but with the Spirit – provided the Spirit of God is living inside you, for anyone who doesn't have the Spirit of the Messiah doesn't belong to him" (Romans 8:9 CJB).

After the Gentiles in Acts 10 are regenerated, Peter announces for them to go through *T'zilah* (water baptism). This places the order in Acts 10 as faith, resulting in salvation, followed by water baptism. Now, do you see the problem?

In Acts 2, salvation comes after water baptism. In Acts 10, salvation comes before water baptism. Unless these passages are synchronized, merely asserting one verse against another does violence to the authority of the Scripture. Can there be any justifiable substitute meanings?

"Therefore, if God gave them the same gift as He gave us after we had come to put our trust in the Lord Yeshua the Messiah, who was I to stand in God's way. On hearing these things, they stopped objecting and began to praise God, saying, "This means that God has enabled the Goyim as well to do t'shuvah and have life!" (Acts 11:17-18 CJB).

In this scripture, Peter is explaining to others what happened in Acts 10. Notice, the mikvah isn't mentioned, only the details of regeneration, repentance, faith, and salvation. This process settles the question on the order, but how do you deal with Acts 2:28?

The key to this answer lies in the grammar. The command to repent is in the plural, as is the recommendation to those who receive the forgiveness of sins. ("**All** of you repent so **all** of you can receive forgiveness"). The command to the mikvah is in the singular. "**Each** of you should be baptized." This makes it clear that repentance, not the T'zilah (water baptism), leads to salvation.

The individual's water baptism cannot produce the salvation of the entire group. In Acts 2, Peter's Jews did not go through a water baptism in order to bring about their salvation. They went through water baptism because of salvation. This line of reason also connects with Acts 10; Acts 11; Acts 2:38; Ephesians 1:13-14; and Romans 8:9. Now let us look at the second example.

Faith And Works

The second example deals with faith and works. Paul says you are not justified by works, but by faith. James says you are not justified by faith, but by works. Paul and James both quote Genesis 15:6 to prove their point. This process again asks two questions. How can both Paul and James be right? Which one is wrong?

First, let's discuss Paul and his understanding. Paul starts with Abraham as the father of the faith, and than uses him as an example of an individual God used to communicate truth about the character of faith, forgiveness, and justification.

"What then shall we say Abraham, our forefather according to the flesh, has founded For if Abraham was justified by works, he has something to boast about, but not before God. For what does the Scripture say? 'Abraham believed God, and it was credited to his as righteousness" (Romans 4:1-3 ASV).

The quotation taken from Genesis 15:6 is extremely important! *"Then he believed in the Lord; and He reckoned it to him as righteousness"* (Genesis 15:6 ASV). The word "reckoned" is a banking term. It presents a picture of God applying righteousness to our empty bank account. God reckons Abraham's faith as righteousness, and for him that does not involve works at all. It shows trust in a God who will justify the ungodly to him, and it is "reckoned" as righteousness. Paul's teaching proves it is faith only, or does it?

Now, let us discuss James:

"Was not Abraham our father justified by works, when he offered up Isaac his son on the altar?"

"You see that faith was working with his works, and as a result of the works, faith was perfected; And the Scripture was fulfilled which says, 'And Abraham believed God, and it was reckoned to him as righteousness," and he was called the friend of God. You see that a man is **justified by works, and not by faith** *[emphasis mine] alone"* (James 2:21-24 ASV).

I repeat: Paul says that you are not justified by works but by faith. James seems to say in these scriptures that you are not justified by faith alone, but also by works, and both Paul and James used the same verse of scripture of Genesis 15:6 for their proof text.

If you believe God speaks through the scriptures, you cannot have a disagreement. How would you bring together the two passages?

Two Meanings Of Justification

Paul used one meaning of justification in Romans 4:1-3 while James used a different meaning in James 2:21-24. Both Paul and James quote Abraham, but they quote different periods of his life.

Paul, in Romans 4:1-3, quotes Genesis. 15:6 when God gave Abraham the covenant. James quotes Genesis 22 when Abraham established his righteousness by trusting God and offering his son, Isaac, on the altar, proving himself righteous.

James connects Genesis 22 to mean an outward appearance, or a completion, of his salvation with Genesis 15:6. What is the solution to the problem?

The key to reconciling the scriptures in this case is the word "justified" has two meanings. One meaning of the word "justify" is to **give righteousness** while another meaning is to **prove to be righteous**. Paul is dealing with the root of salvation, applying faith, and James is dealing with the fruit of salvation, applying trust.

There is a distinction between when God justifies a man and when a man justifies himself.

When you hear the words, "justify yourself," you are being asked to justify your actions, proving something about the nature of your actions. When God justifies a man, He doesn't show them something. He gives them something: righteousness. Having a strong understanding of the Word helps, but what would you do if challenged?

If you are in your battlefields, fighting the strongholds in your life, the attack for your faith will come, ninety percent of the time, from those whom you love. The experiences existing between you and your loved ones allow for stronger weapons of adversity to be fired at the bull's eye target placed on you. Your trust in God is the target. If handled wrong, you may win the battle but lose the war. How do you increase your faith?

VII FAITH'S LADDER OF TRUST

"Never be afraid to trust an unknown future to a known God"

(Carrie Ten Boon – Dutch Evangelist, 1892-1983)

VII. FAITH'S LADDER OF TRUST

—✸—

> *"For in it the righteousness of God is being revealed from faith to faith; as it is written, 'But the righteous man shall live by faith.'"* (Romans 1:17 ASV)

THE SEVEN APPLICATIONS

Strong's Concordance (4102), and *Vines Expository Dictionary of New Testament Words* define faith as "A firm conviction of the truthfulness of God."[17] Romans 1:17 say that you go *"from Faith to Faith."* This shows a progression of degrees to a person's faith. If there is a progression, it means you can go up or down. This same progression can be seen in the tabernacle with steps from the altar of sacrifice to the Holy of Holies.

In the Word of God, there are seven levels of faith, which allow you to climb the rungs of the ladder of trust.

It also has seven life applications that can be applied to the believer in Yeshua. The life applications are conversion or repentance, separation, the study of God's word and fellowship, your testimony, prayer, complete surrender, and then the anointing, which produces victory in a person's life.

As a believer, climb the ladder of trust, move *'from faith to faith'* as you go through the tabernacle, and apply these seven life applications in your life.

THE ALTAR OF SACRIFICE / COMMON FAITH

The purpose of **common faith** is to bring you into the Kingdom and it represents conversion or repentance.

"To Titus, mine own son after the **common faith** *[emphasis mine]: Grace, mercy, and peace from God the Father and the Lord* <u>Yeshua the Messiah</u> *[my translation] our Savior"* (Titus 1:4 KJV).

The first rung on the ladder of trust is called *"common faith,"* and lines up with the altar of sacrifice in the outer court of the tabernacle. The first article of furniture after passing through the eastern gate (which I call *"the whoever gate,"*) was the altar of sacrifice.[18] The word *"altar"* signifies *"to lift up."*[19] The altar was the place of the substitute sacrifice and the place where a person meets God. The priests sacrificed various offerings to God. Some offerings were for their own sins, and some for the sins of the people.

The blood of the animal was poured out at the base of the altar, and, depending on the type of offering, the body was consumed upon the altar itself. It was a place of death. It stood between the gate and the approach to the tabernacle. It barred the way to everyone who would come. There was no approach to the tabernacle except by the way of this altar. Until a person stops at this altar, applies the blood, and accepts the sacrifice as a substitute, there is no further progress. The altar served as both the *way* to God and a *barrier* to God.[20]

Please understand God's perspective in the Bible. In Ezekiel 18:4, God says, *"All souls are Mine... the soul who sins will die"* (NSV). The penalty of sin is death. This is also recorded in Romans 6:23.

Here is the legal position: you belong to God. He made you, and you are His by right. However, you have done your own thing, attempting to live your own life without God. You have sinned. You can and will rationalize that you are not so bad, and compare your lifestyle with others, but God does not grade on a scale. In God's eyes, everything matters, every little sin.

According to the righteous requirement of the instructions of the Torah, you should die for your sin. However, God, through His grace, gave a provision:

"The Life of the Flesh (of a burnt offering / sacrifice) is in the blood, and I have given it to you on the altar to make atonement for your souls; for it is the Blood by reason of the life that makes atonement" (Leviticus. 17:11 KJV).

So, either you must die, or the offering can die in your place. It is a life for a life. If the offering dies, then through its life-blood, there is atonement (at-one-ment) for your soul, and restoration to the God to whom you belong. *"He shall lay his hand on the head of the burnt offering, that it may be accepted for him to made atonement on his behalf"* (Leviticus 1:4 NASB).

This is God's way, His provision. Was this undeserved to the animal? Yes, but it is because you have been unjust towards God that this offering becomes necessary. This is the meaning of faith: Believing in God's provision when you can do nothing for yourself.

You are called *"sheep."* A lamb was burnt at the altar of sacrifice every morning and every evening (Exodus 29:38-42).

The normal destiny of any sheep entering into the tabernacle was certain death. However, Yeshua laid down His life in your place, His sheep.

This altar was made by man, but designed by God. When completed, the Torah says that God ignited the wood upon the altar by fire that fell directly from heaven, and not by human hands (Leviticus 9:24).

The Book of Jonah (Jonah 2:9), read on the fast of Yom Kippur, shows that salvation is entirely and exclusively in the hands of the Lord. No human effort, human help, or human contribution was made to start the fire on this altar; so, also, salvation must be by the grace of God, apart from any human help, merit, religion, or works. To do otherwise meant certain death, as in the case of Nadab and Abihu, who, in an act of religious zeal, died during the actual act of worshipping God (Leviticus 10:1-2). This was God's method of showing His approval, or disapproval, upon an acceptable sacrifice.[21]

The altar of sacrifice had four horns mounted on the each of its four corners. Horns, in Scripture, are symbolic of great power. These horns pointed to the four directions. The first letters of the four directions are "N-E-W-S," - good news.[22]

Not only was the altar of sacrifice the largest piece of furniture, but also it was the first in the order of seven as the priest entered the tabernacle to worship. It was the starting point, the beginning of man's approach to God. Ignoring this altar of sacrifice barred all further progress.[23]

The first step in your walk is *conversion* for the Gentile, and *repentance* for the Jewish person. This is accomplished by trust in God, through faith. This is the first and bottom rung of the ladder of trust. It is called "***common faith***," and is used to bring you into the kingdom of God. You cannot continue until you reach this first rung.

Once here, after your offering, your trust grows, your faith increases, and you can move to the next rung.

THE LAVER / LITTLE FAITH

The second rung is called **little faith**, and can be represented by the second piece of furniture in the outer court of the tabernacle: the laver. The purpose of *little faith* is to learn to increase your trust in God and His word in your life.

This life application represents separation. It is here where you are separated to God by *T'zilah* (water baptism) "*And he said unto them, 'Why are ye fearful, O ye of Little Faith?'*" (Matthew 8:26 KJV)

After the altar, the priest will go to the laver of cleansing. The laver was a washbasin mounted on a base, and stood in the outer court. Made of brass, it was kept filled with clean water. Its function was the washing of the hands and feet of the priests as they ministered in the tabernacle. It speaks of the sanctifying power of the Word of God. Water is symbolic of the Word of God by which you are cleansed and sanctified.[24]

The laver was the only piece of furniture where the dimensions were not given.[25] God commanded that every time the priest approached the altar or the tabernacle he must wash at the laver. What was the reason? The priest became defiled with every step he took, even when he was in God's service.[26] The service of the Lord was an exacting service. The Scripture says, "*They that bear the vessels of the Lord must [emphasis mine] be clean*" (Isaiah 52:11). Washing the hands and feet with the water in the laver did this cleansing. The hands speak of service, the feet of walk and conduct.[27]

The laver represents separation from the world, the flesh, and from things that defile us by the washing of the water by the Word. God warned Moses in Exodus 30:20-21 that if the priests did not wash they would die.

It is a serious requirement that you wash as you come to handle any of the things of the Lord. Why?

Those who believe in Yeshua are considered priests. Read the Word of God:

"*But you are a chosen race, a royal priesthood, a holy nation [emphasis mine], A People for God's own possession [emphasis mine], that you may proclaim the excellencies of Him who has called you out of darkness into His marvelous Light*" (I Peter 2:9 KJV).

And again, *"and He has made us to be a kingdom, priests to His God and Father – to Him be glory and the dominion forever and ever, Amen"* (Revelation 1:6 ASV).

You wash in the laver two ways:

The first is by going through *T'zilah,* or water baptism, after conversion or repentance (Acts 22:16), and the second is through the washing of the laver of your mind in the Word (Ephesians 5:26; John 13:8-10; 15:8). This is in accordance to the pattern in Exodus 29:39, which is, at least, two times a day, morning and evening.

At this point, you have been set apart for God. The word, *"holy"* or *"sanctified"* means *"set apart."* The Scriptures say:

"But you have cleansed yourselves, you have been set apart for God, you have come to be counted righteous through the power of the Lord Yeshua the Messiah and the Spirit of our God" (I Corinthians 6:11 CJB).

When you reach this point in your walk, your trust has grown, and you have stepped on the second rung of the ladder of trust. It is on this rung, through the water of separation, you are learning to increase your trust in God. This is called **"little faith."** When you feel safe in this rung, you are ready to take hold of the third rung.

THE TABLE OF SHEWBREAD / TEMPORARY FAITH

The purpose of **temporary faith** is to show faith until tested, and the life application is the study of the Word of God and Fellowship.

"Those on the rocky soil are those, when, they hear, receive the word with joy; and these have no firm root; they believe for a while, and in the time of temptation fall away" (Luke 8:13 ASV).

The third rung, called **"temporary faith,"** is the most fragile, and is represented by the table of shewbread in the

Holy Place of the tabernacle. This is the most critical of all the rungs. Without the fellowship of other believers, and applied knowledge (wisdom) of the Word of God, the person will go down the ladder of trust instead of advancing to the next rung.

The parable of the sower is recorded in three of the four Gospels.

"and others fell upon the rocky places, where they had not much earth: and straightway they sprang up, because they had no deepness of earth: and when the sun was risen, they were scorched; and because they had no root, they withered away" (Matt 13:5-6 ASV).

"And these in like manner are they that are sown upon the rocky places, who, when they have heard the word, straightway receive it with joy; and they have no root in themselves, but endure for a while; then, when tribulation or persecution ariseth because of the word, straightway they stumble" (Mark 4:16-17 ASV).

"And some fell upon a rock; and as soon as it was sprung up, it withered away, because it lacked moisture" (Luke 8:6 KJV).

The explanation of the parable of the sower is found in Matthew 13:21:

"Yet hath he not root in himself, but dureth for a while: for when tribulation or persecution ariseth **because of the word** *[emphasis mine], by and by he is offended"* (KJV).

This is temporary faith. It is on this rung of trust that your faith can go down or up. It will be on the basis of offense because of the Word.

Two words require definition: belief and disbelief. Belief, in Greek "pis-yoo-o," has three meanings: *"to have faith, to entrust or commit, or credit."* In Hebrew, the word "aw-man" means, *"to build up."*

The word disbelief, in Greek "ap-is-the-o" has two meanings: *"to refuse to believe, which by refusing to believe you are disobeying"* and *"disobey, to be disobedient."*

Do you believe Yeshua is the Son of God, and based only on this belief, you are saved? Scriptures cannot lie. If this is your belief, explain these Scriptures:

"Thou believest that God is one; thou doest well: the demons also believe, and shudder" (James 2:19 ASV).

*"He that believeth on the Son hath eternal life; but he that **obeyeth not** [emphasis mine] the Son shall not see life, but the wrath of God abideth on him"* (John 3:36 ASV).

There are five steps, up or down, every believer might take with its congregation. A husband and wife might take these same steps with each other. Every believer will take four of these steps. The first step is *"expectation,"* also known as the honeymoon period. Depending on how long this period exists, you will come to the next step, *"reality."* This step, quickly, will take you to the third step, *"disillusion."*

Here, at the *"disillusion"* step, you are at **"temporary faith,"** and your faith is being tested. You can go down or up. The downward step is called *"license,"* where you try, in different ways, to influence your expectation into reality, forcing a breakup.

The upward step is called *"graceful love,"* where you accept the reality and move forward. If you are at temporary faith, which step will you take?

The table of shewbread in the Holy Place of the tabernacle had a crown, in Hebrew called "ketar," that is called *"the crown of kingship"* in the Talmud (Yoma 76b). It represents Yeshua as Israel's defender as well as its provider.

Both the table and the bread in the tabernacle point to Yeshua. On the table were placed twelve loaves of bread, six in two separate rows.[28] There are twelve major doctrines in the *Brit Hadashah*, lining up with the twelve loaves. They are: salvation (Acts 4:12), justification (Romans 5:1), water immersion (Matthew 28:19), sanctification (1 Thessalonians 4:3), baptism in the *Ruach Hakodesh* (Matthew 3:11), laying on of hands (Hebrews 6:2), second coming of the Messiah (Acts 1:11-12), the resurrection of the dead (Hebrews 6:2), judgment of the righteous (1 Peter 4:5), judgment of the unrighteous (Revelation 20:11), eternal life for the righteous (John 3:15), and, the last, eternal punishment for the unrighteous (Revelation 20:14).

The bread was flavored with frankincense. This was the food of the priest. Around this table, the priests worshipped and enjoyed fellowship daily, on the basis of the blood of the sacrificed animal that was slain on the altar. The bread speaks of Yeshua, as the living bread. (John 6:35,48,51) The table pointed to Yeshua, our sustainer, and the bread on the table was His body. The table was the center of fellowship for the priest, and the bread was the living Word.

You are a priest, ministering unto the Lord. As a priest, you are to seek fellowship with other believers in the Holy Place.[29] This act represents the "assembling of the saints" in Scripture. There is no *Rambo* or *Lone Ranger* in this group.

There is no believer so advanced in the things of *God* that he can go without the fellowship and blessings of the believers who gather around the table of the Lord.[30]

The foundation of this fellowship was the table of shewbread. Since the table is Yeshua, all true fellowship must be around the person and the work of the Lord. Remember that the bread on the table had frankincense, which represents the *Ruach Hakodesh*, and was the only thing placed on the table. That was all that was necessary for health and life. Do you know how the priests were required to eat at this table?

They must eat standing up. There were no chairs in the tabernacle. The house of God was not a place of ease and entertainment, but a place of work and service. They ate their bread, standing on their feet, ready to serve the people.[31] Any moment, the order might come to move on, and they must be ready to pack up and leave. You, also, must gather in the fellowship of believers, waiting for orders to move on.[32]

Bread is wheat, ground into flour, and baked in a heated oven. Bread is the result of a process of death and suffering. The crushing of the wheat speaks of Gethsemane, and the burning heat the oven speaks of Calvary. This fulfills the promise of Scripture. It reads: "*And Yeshua [my translation] said unto them, 'I am the Bread of Life. He that comes to me shall never hunger; and he that believes on me, shall never thirst*" (John 6:35 KJV).

It is here you enter the place of fellowship with other believers in the assembly. You are fed on Yeshua, the Word of God who is the Bread of Life, at the table of fellowship. It is here your faith is really tested. Through *Bible study* and *fellowship*, your trust increases, and you can go up the next rung on the ladder. If not done, your trust becomes shaky, and you will step down a rung. This rung is called "***temporary faith***," faith until tested.

THE MENORAH / STRONG FAITH

If you have advanced up, not stepped down, you are on the fourth rung of the ladder of trust called "***strong faith.***" It is represented by the menorah in the Holy Place. At this level, you will refuse defeat. You drive home this point through the continuous study of God's Word, and the word of your testimony, which is your fourth life application.

"*Who against hope* **believed in hope** *[emphasis mine], that he might become the father of many Nations; according to that which was spoken, 'So shall thy seed be' And being not weak in Faith he* **considered not** *[emphasis mine] his own body now dead, when he was about an hundred years old, neither yet the deadness of Sara's womb: He* **staggered not** *[emphasis mine] at the promise of God through unbelief; but was* **strong in faith** *[emphasis mine], giving glory to God And being* **fully persuaded** *[emphasis mine] that,* *what he had promised, he was able to perform and therefore it was imputed to him for righteousness*" (Romans 4:18-22 KJV).

Abraham refused defeat, and at the age of one hundred, and Sarah at the age of ninety, Isaac was born. This miracle came about because of Abraham's trust in G-d.

The menorah, or candlestick, was a symbol of a person. There is a personal pronoun applied to it. God said in Exodus 25:31 that the menorah was to be made from pure gold, along with **his** shaft, and **his** branches.[33] The menorah represents Yeshua the Messiah who said, "*...I am the Light of the World*" (John 9:5).

The golden menorah stood on the south side of the tabernacle opposite the table of shewbread, with the altar of incense closer to the veil. The light of the menorah was indispensable in the service of the priests. There were no windows provided in the pattern given for the tabernacle. Not a single ray of light was allowed to come from the outside by the light of nature.[34]

The oil in the menorah represents the *Ruach Hakodesh*. Ephesians 4:4 state that there is only one Spirit, yet the Scripture speaks of the "*seven spirits of God*" (Revelation 3:1, 4:5; 5:6).

In Isaiah 11:2, the Scripture states that *the Ruach Hakodesh* has seven divine attributes that was given to Yeshua in its fullness: the Spirit of the Lord, the Spirit of wisdom, the Spirit of understanding, the Spirit of counsel, the Spirit of might, the Spirit of knowledge, and the Spirit of the tear of the Lord.

As you consume God's Word, you will receive knowledge, understanding, and wisdom. Paul prayed in Ephesians 1:18 that the eyes of your understanding should be open. Light expels darkness, and truth from the God's Word creates light in the human mind. This light is called understanding.

The menorah was the only source of light by which the priests was to serve in the tabernacle. This light points to Yeshua. *"Your word is a lamp to my feet and a light to my path"* (Psalm 119:105 ASV). The believer is only to walk by the light of the Word of God.[35]

The menorah was fed by the pure olive oil, and was specially ordered, and prepared for God (Exodus 27:20). This oil was also used for the anointing of the priests.[36] The word *"Messiah"* in Hebrew means, literally *"The Anointed One."*

Isaiah 61:1 was the verse Yeshua used to start His ministry, and was also said by Peter in his own words *"How God anointed Yeshua from Natzeret with the Ruach Hakodesh and with power; how Yeshua went about doing good and healing all the people oppressed by the adversary, because God was with Him"* (Acts 10:38 CJB).

The menorah has seven branches, one center branch, with three branches on each side. The center branch, known as "the servant branch," was used to light the other branches. Yeshua represents the vine, the believers the branches (John 15:5). In addition, the flames of the six side branches pointed toward the center branch.

This fourth step on the ladder of trust, called **strong faith**, refuses defeat. You stand on this rung, showing your trust, by letting your light shine in testimony.

"Ye are the light of the world. A city set on a hill cannot be hid. Neither do men light a lamp, and put it under the bushel, but on the stand, and it shineth unto all that are in the house. Even so let your light shine before men; that they may see your good works, and glorify your Father who is in heaven" (Matthew 5:14-16 ASV).

As the oil of the *Ruach Hakodesh* feeds the branches of the menorah, allow God to light the menorah in your heart. It will let your light shine on the darkness. In addition, it will create a spiritual wildfire in you, burning out everything that hinders the work you were sent to do. Bring in the light to your walk. You can then go to the fifth rung on the ladder of trust.

THE ALTAR OF INCENSE / CREATIVE FAITH

The incense altar in the Holy Place represents the fifth rung, also called "**great faith**." This rung of faith understands the authority of God and believes God's Word will not return void. Confession will always follow the Word, and prayer is its life application.

"*When <u>Yeshua</u> [my translation] heard it, he marveled, and said unto them that followed, 'Verily I say unto you, I have not found so **great faith** [emphasis mine], no, not in Israel*'" (Matthew 8:10 KJV).

The altar of incense was the tallest piece of furniture in the Holy Place, and speaks of the highest act of worship.[37] Burning incense represented the prayers and priestly intercession of God's people going up before the throne of God (Psalm 141:2). The need for the intercession was constant. Why? The priests were defiled daily by contact with the earth on which they walked. They needed confession and intercession at the golden altar of incense.

There are, according to Jewish tradition, eleven spices to produce the incense. Five are listed in the written Torah, and the rest are found in the Talmud (Tractate "*Keritot*"). They are: balsam, clove, galbanum, frankincense, myrrh, cassia, spikeard, saffron, costus, aromatic bark, and cinnamon. These spices were offered on both the morning and evening sacrifices. On the day before Yom Kippur, the incense would be ground again; thereby producing "*the finest of the fine.*"

The eleven spices connect eleven types of prayer with the incense. They are the prayer for confessing our sins (1 John 1:9), the prayer for confessing our faith (James 5:16), the prayer of agreement (Matthew 18:19), the prayer of faith for the sick (James 5:15), the prayer of binding (Matthew

16:19), the prayer of loosing (Matt 16:19), the praying in the spirit (Ephesians 6:18), the praying in the Spirit with understanding (1 Corinthians 14:15), the prayer of thanksgiving (Philippians 4:6), the prayer of intercession (1 Tim 2:1), and the prayer for general supplication (Philippians 4:6).

This golden altar is a condemnation of any claim to perfection in the priest's walk. The incense, rising before the veil, was a constant reminder to the priest that he still had the old nature, that he still came short, and that he still needed intercession at the altar of incense.

The highest office of the believer is intercessory prayer. Prayer is the process that activates the power of God. As the incense was offered on the altar with exact measurements, so the prayers must be offered with the knowledge and understanding of the authority of God.

God is more pleased with our worship than our service. When the praises go up, the blessings come down.

The incense offering was the most precious part of the tabernacle's service in the eyes of God, and every priest hoped to have the honor of conducting this service. It was permitted only as a once in a lifetime opportunity. It was said that God rewards the one who had the privilege to offer the incense with wealth and prosperity forever, in this world and the next.

There can be no acceptable service until you have stopped to worship, first, at the altar of incense. It is by the offering on the altar of sacrifice you are saved, but it is by the incense on the altar of incense you are kept.[38]

The priest at this altar does not pray for non-believers. The priest at the altar of incense is powerless to do a single thing for the unbeliever until the unbeliever first comes to the altar of sacrifice, with repentance.[39]

Prayer without faith is worthless, and the person who comes to God praying without faith accomplishes nothing.[40] There is only one way, a personal faith in the finished work of Yeshua. On this rung of the ladder of trust, through prayer, you truly understand and trust the authority of God.

God's Word will not return void on this rung. This rung, called *"creative faith,"* is better known as *"great faith."* You cannot go to the next rung on the ladder without understanding and trusting the authority of God. Only by accepting God's authority on your life, can you go behind the veil to the Ark of the Covenant.

THE ARK OF THE COVENANT / ACTIVE FAITH

The Ark of the Covenant in the Holy of Holies represents this sixth rung on the ladder of trust, called *"active faith."* The purpose of active faith is to show the power of confessing the Word, and its life application is full surrender.

"But be ye doers of the Word, and not hearers only, deceiving your own selves."

"For if any be a hearer of the Word, and not a doer, he is like a man beholding his natural face in a glass: For he beholdeth himself, and goeth his way, and straightway forgetteth what manner of man he was; But who so looketh into the perfect law of liberty [emphasis mine], and continueth therein, he being not a forgetful hearer, but a doer of the work, this man shall be blessed in his deed" (James 1:22-25 KJV).

The Ark of the Covenant was the most important piece of furniture in the entire tabernacle.[41] It was the first piece of the tabernacle God told Moses to build. The ark also wore a golden crown (Exodus 25:11). Crowns are for kings to wear and are symbols of sovereignty and power.[42] The crown on the ark was called *"the crown of Torah."*

According to Hebrews 9:4, Moses placed three important items inside the ark: the golden pot of manna representing salvation (John 6:35), the tablets of the law representing sanctification (John 17:17), the rod of Aaron that budded representing the power of the *Ruach Hakodesh* (Numbers

161

17) (See Appendix 1). These three items represent the three blessings every believer receives into their inner spirit when they arrive at the ark.

However, there is the warning. The Bible states two items were removed from the ark in the time of Solomon (1 Kings 8:9): the manna (*salvation*), and the rod of Aaron (The *Ruach Hakodesh power*). When you stop ministering salvation, and omit the power and moving of the *Ruach Hakodesh*, you are left with the Law.

The Bible says in 1 Corinthians 3:6, *"For the letter killeth, but the spirit giveth life."* The best example is Solomon, who, in his later years departed from the Lord. Without the manna (*salvation*) and the rod (*Ruach Hakodesh power*), you will depart from the faith.

Many in Yeshua's time were masters of the Law, but were missing the *Ruach Hakodesh* power. Consider the prophetic significance: the Bible tells us that in the last days the *Ruach Hakodesh* will be removed in some congregations.

"Holding to a form of Godliness, although they have denied its power; Avoid such men as these" (2 Timothy 3:5 ASV). They will have the form but no power.

Yeshua has three offices: prophet, priest, and king. In the court at the brazen altar of sacrifice, you see Yeshua as prophet. A prophet is one who comes from God with God's message for man.[43] Yeshua came to bring you God's message of grace and mercy.

In the Holy Place, you see Yeshua as your high priest. A priest is one who intercedes for the people.[44] In the Holy Place, the priest offered the incense on the altar of incense, and Yeshua is, today, interceding for those who believe.

However, behind the veil into the Holy of Holies, you meet Yeshua as your king, whose commands and will are unconditional. Few believers have entered this experience of full surrender, of yielding to Yeshua as King and Lord of their lives with all that they are or possess.[45]

When you enter this experience, the life application of full surrender to the will of God becomes a priority in your life. Bottom-line behavior is created by what you think and speak. What you speak is connected to what you do (James 1:26). You meditate and speak, than you can do the Word of God (Joshua 1:8).

The tabernacle had three compartments: an outer court – the place of sacrifice; an inner room called the Holy Place – the place of worship; then the innermost room, the Holy of Holies – the place of communion with God and victory.[46] If you are here, you have reached the sixth rung of the ladder of trust.

This rung, again, is called **active faith.** It is here that you apply the blood by full surrender and confessing the Word of God. This raises your trust in God to a new level, and you, by faith, are climbing the seventh, and final, rung on the ladder of trust.

You are standing on the side of the ark, but the last step – the last rung - places you in the very presence of the *Shchinah,* the glory of God.

THE MERCY SEAT / DIVINE FAITH

There are exactly seven articles of furniture in the tabernacle, two in the court, three in the Holy Place, and two in the Holy of Holies. It has seven pieces of furniture, exactly seven, and no more. Seven is the number of *spiritual perfection.*[47]

The seventh and final rung, called *divine faith*, is represented by the mercy seat. The purpose of divine faith is to receive the full trust and faith of God in your life. It is through this life application, on the mercy seat, that the blood is applied, and you receive victory and the anointing.

*"But the Scripture hath concluded all under sin, that **the promise by faith** [emphasis mine] of <u>Yeshua the Messiah</u> [my*

*translation] might be **given to them that believe [emphasis mine]**"* (Galatians 3:22 KJV).

The Ark of the Covenant was a symbol of the throne of God. The broken tablets of the Law lay in this ark, the throne of God. The ark, by itself, was a throne of judgment.

The veil before the ark barred anyone from coming to God, and the broken law threatened death to all that dared to approach the throne. A provision had to be made for man to be protected from God's *Shchinah,* a pillar of holiness and fire. That provision, given to Moses on the mount, was the mercy seat.

The mercy seat was made of beaten gold. The mercy seat was between God and the broken law. Over the mercy seat, with wings stretched out, stood the cherubim, which were symbols of the holiness of God. [48]

Without the mercy seat, they would be looking down on the broken tablets of the law, and God's holiness would demand the death of the sinner.[49]

On the mercy seat, which also served as the cover of the ark, was sprinkled the blood of a slain animal from the altar of sacrifice.

Once every year, after offering a sacrifice for himself, the priesthood, and the sins of the people, the high priest took the blood in a basin, went past the veil, and entered the Holy of Holies.[50]

He sprinkled the blood upon the mercy seat, over and above the broken law, which called for the judgment of death.[51]

Now, when God came down in the *Shchinah* cloud over the ark, instead of seeing the broken law, He saw, instead, the blood of atonement, and could not exercise the judgment of death because of the broken law. He, Himself, had promised: *"When I see the **blood**, [emphasis mine] I will pass over"* (Exodus 12:13 KJV). By the sprinkling of the blood, the throne of judgment became the throne of mercy.[52]

When the priest killed the red heifer, he dipped his finger in blood and sprinkled it seven times toward the door of the tabernacle (Numbers 19:1-10), and seven times on the mercy seat. Yeshua shed his blood seven times during His suffering: in the Garden of Gethsemane, at the whipping post, when they placed the crown of thorns on His head, when they beat His face, when they pierced His feet, when they pierced His hands, and when they pierced His side.

Without the blood, you will invite immediate death. *"And He (God) smote the men at beth-shemesh **because they looked into the Ark of the Lord**, [emphasis mine] even he smote of the people 50,070 and the people lamented, because the Lord had smitten many of the people with a great slaughter"* (1 Samuel 6:19 KJV).

When the blood is removed, the seat of mercy becomes the seat of judgment. When the high priest went into the Holy of Holies on Yom Kippur, the Day of Atonement, he needed to do nothing except to present and apply the blood. Neither the Bible nor the Talmud records that the high priest ever spoke a single word as he stood in the presence of God. The blood was enough.[53] The blood speaks for you. God says, *"When I **see** [emphasis mine] the blood, I will pass over"* (Exodus 12:13).

You, as a believer, are *"in Yeshua."* You can now come to the throne of grace, not demanding, but boldly, and without fear because of your fixed position and His blood sacrifice. Hebrews 4:16 reads, *"Let us therefore draw near with boldness unto the throne of grace, that we may receive mercy, and may find grace to help us in time of need"* (ASV).

This is also repeated in Hebrews 10:19-22

"Since therefore, brethren, we have confidence to enter into the holy place by the blood of <u>Yeshua</u> [my translation], by a new and living way, which He inaugurated for us through the veil, that is, his flesh; and since we have a great priest over the house of God; let us draw near with a sincere

heart in full assurance of faith, having our hearts sprinkled clean from an evil conscience: and our body washed with pure water" (ASV).

Where is the dwelling place of God now? He dwells in two places.

The Temple In Heaven

When Moses was on the mountain and receiving the instructions for the tabernacle, God gave him specific directives:

"And see that thou make them after their pattern, which hath been showed thee in the mount" (Exodus 25:40 ASV).

This is also repeated in the *Brit Hadashah*:

"who serve that which is a copy and shadow of the heavenly things, even as Moses is warned of God when he is about to make the tabernacle: for, See, saith he, that thou make all things according to the pattern that was showed thee in the mount" (Hcbrews 8:5 ASV).

The reality of the *"pattern and shadow"* was the temple in heaven, where God is dwelling now. Where the heavenly temple is, there is the ark.

"And there was opened the temple of God that is in heaven; and there was seen in his temple the ark of his covenant; and there followed lightnings, and voices, and thunders, and an earthquake, and great hail" (Revelation 11:19).

The Temple In You

God also dwells in a temple on earth. Scripture says you are God's temple.

"Know ye not that ye are a temple of God, and that the Spirit of God dwelleth in you? If any man destroyeth the temple of God, him shall God destroy; for the temple of God is holy, and such are ye" (1 Corinthians 3:16-17 ASV).

The items missing in your ark were replaced through Yeshua. Yeshua gave you back salvation, represented by the bowl of manna. He also gave you back the resurrection life and the power of the *Ruach Hakodesh*, represented by Aaron's rod. The tables of the covenant have been changed. They no longer are written in stone, but written on your heart. Does this mean you no longer have to follow the *Torah*? God forbid, No! (See Appendix 3).

Your past can prevent you from reaching the Holy of Holies. Your inability of forgiving yourself will keep you from experiencing the fullness of God's presence. God has forgiven you. He desires your fellowship, and will "*tabernacle*" with you.

You must forgive yourself, and change by the renewing of your mind. One of the best examples of this process in Scripture is the parable of the prodigal son, as recorded in Luke 15.

This parable had a profound effect on an artist named Rembrandt. When he was a young man, he painted the picture called *The Prodigal Son*. It was a self-portrait. There were things in his young life he could not forgive, so he painted himself as the prodigal son.

Later in his life, he painted another picture called, *The Return of the Prodigal Son*. In this picture, he again created a self-portrait. This time he was the father. He had learned to forgive himself. Because of it, he was able to forgive others. If you were Rembrandt, which picture would be your self-portrait?

This is the last rung on the ladder of trust. On this rung, your trust has grown to the point where you receive your reward. It is called **divine faith**, or the faith of God. It is on this rung that you receive **victory and the anointing** because of your trust in God.

It is here, at the mercy seat, where you meet the presence of God. It is here where God's priorities become yours. His priorities are: the honor of His name, the love for His word, and the advancement of His Kingdom.

Now, let me ask you some questions: Are these priorities yours? If yes, how are you doing it? You developed the trust, but whose faith climbed the ladder? Grace always flows downward, never uphill, and grace is always followed by mercy.

It is God's grace and mercy that enables your trust to grow, and allows you to go *"from faith to faith"* (Romans 1:17). Left on your own, you would have no reason, or desire, to even go to the first rung of the ladder.

Are there any examples in scripture that can teach you how to go *"from faith to faith?"* Yes. Let's look at two examples: the woman with the issue of blood, as recorded in Matthew 9, and David, when he fought Goliath, as recorded in 1 Samuel 17.

VIII   THE LADDER OF TRUST AND YOUR CHOICE

*"Though the mills of God grind slowly;
they grind exceeding small."*

Friedrich Von Logau (1604 – 1655)

VIII.   THE LADDER OF TRUST AND YOUR CHOICE

———❧———

> *"Yeshua said to her, "Didn't I tell you that if you keep trusting, you will see the glory of God?"* (John 11:40 CJB)

THE FOUR STEPS FOR HEALING

Mark 5:25-34 tells the story of a woman who had a hemorrhage for 12 years. It is very easy to undervalue this section of Scripture. It is placed between healing the man possessed of the legion of devils, and the raising of Jairus' daughter from the dead.

The story is recorded in three places: Matthew 9:20-22; Mark 5:25-34; and Luke 7:42-48.

The Greek word that is translated "hemorrhage" or "flow of blood" in this Scripture is also used in the Septuagint in Leviticus 15:25-27.

"And if a woman have an issue of her blood many days out of the time of her separation, or if it run beyond the time of her separation; all the days of the issue of her uncleanness shall be as the days of her separation: she shall be unclean."

"Every bed whereon she lieth all the days of her issue shall be unto her as the bed of her separation: and whatsoever she sitteth upon shall be unclean, as the uncleanness of her separation."

"And whosoever toucheth those things shall be unclean, and shall wash his clothes, and bathe himself in water, and be unclean until the even" (KJV).

This woman, according to these Scriptures, was considered unclean. To receive her healing this woman went through the process of four steps. These four steps are required to get to the faith and trust of the seventh rung.

She Desired.

This woman's distress was more than just the physical hurt. She suffered from the social customs of her day, the psychological torment of no cure. The worst was the spiritual burden because of the Torah's statement about her condition. She could not touch anyone without making him unclean, and it prevented her from worshipping God. She would not be allowed to enter the temple, offer sacrifices, or have her sins declared forgiven by the priest.

"And had suffered many things of many physicians, and had spent all that she had, and was nothing bettered, but rather grew worse" (Mark 5:26 KJV).

At this time, she has not yet touched the ladder of trust; but she wanted a change in her life. She desired healing. Her desire was so strong she was willing to go against the Torah and the social norms of her society to be healed. She could not be in the crowd of people because of her condition.

She Heard

"When she had heard of <u>Yeshua</u> [my translation], came in the press behind, and touched his garment" (Mark 5:27 –KJV).

At this point in her life, she hears something about Yeshua. We do not know what it was. We do know that Yeshua demonstrated His authority as the agent of the kingdom seven times before she received her healing. They were: the healing of the leper (Matthew 8:1-4), the healing of the Centurion's servant (Matthew 8:5-13), the healing of Peter's mother-in-law and the sick of Capernaum (Matthew 8:14-17), the calming of the wind and waves (Matthew 8:23-27), the exorcism of the demoniacs (Matthew 8:28-34), and the healing of the paralytic at Capernaum, Yeshua's home city (Matthew 9:1-8).

Hearing that Yeshua was a man of God and a healer caused trust in God, and then faith, to be born. She was on the second rung (learning to trust God), and reaching for the third rung (temporary faith).

She Believed

"She shared the ancient view that the healer's own person was potent and that his clothing, or even his shadow, could serve as bearers of his power"[54]

This statement may be true, but there could have been another reason.

"For she said, If I may touch but his clothes I shall be whole." (Mark 5:28 KJV)

According to Matthew 9:20, it was a specific part of His garment she was attempting to touch. At the hem of His garment would have been the *Tzitzis*.

The prophet Malachi said, *"But unto you that fear My name shall the Sun of righteousness arise with healing in His wings"* (Malachi 4:2 KJV). The Biblical Hebrew word for both "wings" and "corners" is *"canaphim."* Numbers 15:38-41 commands the children of Israel to tie the *"Tzitzis"* on the *"canaphim"* (corners / wings) of the garment.

As her faith increased that Yeshua was the one prophesied as the *"Sun of righteousness,"* she was certain that by grabbing hold of His wings (the garment corners where the *Tzitzis* was attached) she would be healed.

Her trust and faith continued to grew by the power of the word she heard. She went from the third rung, and reached for the fourth rung of her ladder of trust (refuse defeat).

Her faith was more than just words. She believed it so strongly that she risked breaking all the societal and ritual rules about cleanliness to follow what she believed to be true. This explains why, when she already had her healing, she was frightened when she was discovered.

She Acted

Whatever the woman's doubts were, she let go of them and she acted on her faith. An imperfect, little faith, acted on, is better than great faith unsupported by deeds. Her faith and trust grew to the extent that she was willing to act on the desire by the power of the word she heard. She thought *"If I touch...(His Tzitzis)...I will get well."* All doubt was gone. What was her reward?

"And straightway the fountain of her blood was dried up; and she felt in her body that she was healed of that plague." (Mark 5:29 KJV)

She understood the Authority of God (fifth rung); and it took her into the Holy of Holies (sixth rung – full surrender) where she received her healing (seventh rung – the anointing or reward).

The Testimony

How important is your testimony? Had Yeshua not stopped and said, *"Who touched my clothes?"* (Mark 5:30 KJV), no one would have known of the miracle except Yeshua and the woman. When she realized Yeshua knew everything, she told him the whole truth, telling how Yeshua had done what medical science, at that time, could not. Yeshua made it clear that it was her faith that healed her, not magic in his clothing. Faith cures where medical skill has failed for twelve years.

This story is also recorded in Matthew 9:20-22. The prologue to this story can be missed. Let's take a look at Matthew 14:34-36

"And when they were gone over, they came into the land of Gennesaret. And when the men of that place had knowledge of him, they sent out into all that country round about, and brought unto him all that were diseased; And besought him that they might only touch the hem of his garment [His Tzitzis]: and as many as touched were made perfectly whole" (KJV).

There are no written Scriptures explaining why they had knowledge of Yeshua, or how they knew to touch His *Tzitzis* to be healed. A possible reason could be that the woman told them while explaining how she would finally be allowed, after twelve years, to attend the local synagogue services.

DAVID AND THE LADDER OF TRUST

Have you ever faced a giant in your life?

The ladder of trust can apply in scripture with the example of David. 1 Samuel chapter 17 (KJV), tell the story of David and Goliath. It is a story of the faith of David and the fear of Goliath. Hope is desire plus expectancy. Fear is expectancy less desire. Despair is desire less expectancy. The story of David and Goliath has all three: hope, fear, and despair.

David's Giant

When the spies checked out the land of Israel, they gave a bad report. Part of that report was giants in the land. Goliath came from that area. Goliath was between nine feet six inches and nine feet nine inches tall. He weighed between four hundred fifty and five hundred pounds.

Goliath had a helmet of brass on his head, and his entire body was covered with jointed plates of metal, which looked like fish scales. The weight of his armor was between one hundred twenty five and one hundred ninety four pounds. The fish scales of the armor made sense. The god of the Philistines was Dagon, the fish god and Goliath was a religious man. He had a brass shin-piece of armor on his legs. He had a plate of brass covering his chest. He had a large spear, with the spear's head made of iron weighing between fifteen and twenty three pounds.

There were two types of shields during the time of David. One type of shield was a small round shield worn on the arm. The other shield looked like a door, and was so heavy it required a shield bearer to carry it. Goliath had the latter.

Five Attitudes of a Giant Killer

There are five principles of a giant killer, and David possessed all five of them.

The first principle is to be consistent in routine things. After David was anointed as the next king of Israel, he continued doing what he was doing. He took care of sheep. When his father, Jesse, wanted him to run an errand, taking food to his brothers, he obeyed. David was faithful in the routine things, knowing he was going to be the next king. His ego was in check.

The second principle is to be challenged by impossible things. King Saul was challenged for 40 days, and did not respond. As king, it should have been his job to fight Goliath, but he was a coward.

As David was talking to his brothers, he heard Goliath's challenge. David started asking questions. The first question David asked was about the incentive program being offered to kill Goliath. David understood a very important principle. The God of Saul was also the God of David, and God rewards those who seek Him.

The third principle is to be committed despite discouragement. As you climb the ladder of trust, you will learn two values. The first value is the greater the challenge, the greater the faith. The second value is the greater the commitment, the greater the attack that will come.

When David committed himself to fight Goliath, the attack came from his own family, and King Saul. If a person cannot be the champion, they try to discourage others. As you become more committed, be prepared for the same discouragements coming from your loved ones and those who have authority over you. When you are going through a fight, you cannot be discouraged. This will move you down the ladder of trust, not up.

The fourth principle is to be courageous in the Lord. Verse 37 reads, *"The Lord delivered me out of the paw of the lion and out of the paw of the bear, He will deliver me out of the hand of this Philistine..."* David was not bragging. God has been on his side in the past and David was bringing it into remembrance. Past victories will help you win future victories. By bringing in your strength in the Lord, you, like David, become powerful.

With these words, where was David on the ladder of trust? David is on the fourth rung of **great faith.** He refuses defeat. When you get to this rung, follow the example of David. In verses 38 and 39, Saul wanted David to use his armor, but David refused. You cannot use other people's faith to climb the ladder. It will not fit. Genuine success in overcoming difficulties and obstacles in life involves where you place your trust and confidence. David uses his own weapons, a staff, sling, and five smooth stones.

If David had **great faith**, why did he pick up five smooth stones? It is believed that Goliath had four brothers. Scripture does record, at least, one of them. It is recorded in 1 Chronicles 20:5.

"And there was war with the Philistines again, and Elhanan the son of Jair killed Lahmi the brother of Goliath

the Gittite, the shaft of whose spear was like a weaver's beam" (ASV).

The fifth principle is to be confident in the spirit. The courage and power to face and conquer the many difficulties that confront you every day are the result of living and acting from trust and confidence in the Lord.

Goliath has been asking for six weeks, morning and night, for someone to fight him. Now a kid with no armor is facing him. Goliath was angry and cursed David.

Again, David is on the fourth rung of **great faith.** He refuses defeat. Does he stay there? No! The most important detail about Goliath is not his size, his armor, his race, nor his challenge. It is in the word, "defy." Goliath used this word six times in this chapter (verses 10, 23, 25, 26, 36, and 45). The Hebrew word means, "to treat with contempt or scorn."

When David saw Goliath curse God, David got angry. Now go the verse 45: *"Then said David to the Philistine, 'Thou comest to me with a sword, and with a spear, and with a shield: but I come to thee in the name of the Lord of Hosts, the God of the armies of Israel, whom you have defiled'"* (KJV).

With these words, David goes up the next rung, **creative faith.** He recognized the authority of God. With the next two verses, verses 46 and 47, David goes to the next rung of the ladder of trust, **active faith.**

Read these verses:

"This day will the Lord deliver thee into mine hand; and I will smite thee, and take thine head from thee; and I will give the carcasses of the host of the Philistines this day unto the fowls of the air, and to the wild beasts of the earth; that all the earth may know that there is a God is Israel. And all this assembly shall know that the Lord saveth not with sword and spear; for the battle is the Lord's, and He will give you into our hands" (1 Samuel 17:46-47 KJV).

The moment of truth has arrived. If God was not who He said He was, David was history.

David does not stop at the sixth rung. God takes David to **divine faith** in verse 49, by giving him the reward of the word he confessed. *"And David put his hand in his bag and took thence a stone, and slang it, and smote the Philistine in the forehead, that the stone sunk into his forehead; and he fell upon his face to the earth"* (KJV).

You could say they had a "meeting of the minds." David is under the anointing of God, and God gives David the victory over the giant, Goliath.

There are three lessons that can be learned from David

The first lesson is to confront the problem. David confronted the problem with Goliath, Saul did not. God will never remove you from your problems but will always make you work through them. It is through this process that you learn to help others.

The second lesson is to cherish your victories. I Samuel 17:54 states that David took the head of Goliath and brought it to Jerusalem, but the weapons of Goliath he put in his tent. Every day he would look at it, reliving the victory. You also must build monuments for God. It helps you remember what God has done for you. Remembering your past victories increases your trust in God, and you will climb the ladder faster.

The third lesson is to concentrate on the goal. The word focus means, "a major point of concentration." It is your vision, or calling, that will give you focus. A clear focus will clarify your vision, or goal. The driving goal David had was to vindicate the glory of God, and he never lost his focus. Do you have the spirit of David?

God had taken David to the top rung of the ladder of trust, but what about Goliath? The Scriptures said that Goliath had faith. Verse 43 reads, *"And the Philistine cursed David **by his gods** [emphasis mine]."* Goliath, because of his belief in his gods made the mistake of defying *"the armies of the living God"* (Verse 45). Again, Goliath had faith but the object of his faith was wrong.

The danger of false doctrines would be like dancing on the *Titanic* while the ship is sinking. The reason false doctrines exist is not because people are ignorant of the facts but they have not learned to think from the right starting point.

Abraham Lincoln said, *"If you look for the bad in a person, expecting to find it, you surely will."* [55]

Once a person presumes a false doctrine, like evolution, is correct, many of the pieces in his thinking are made to fit. If you presume someone associated with a crime is guilty, you are bound to find some pieces of evidence that appear incriminating; but if your suspect produces an airtight alibi, you must rework your presumptions.

If you can attack the person as your defense, you avoid the issue entirely. This is what most people do. It is easier to dismiss any objections to any false doctrine by attacking the messenger than to engage fairly and intelligently the facts in public debate.

Let us summarize the ladder of trust with its life applications:

Common faith	Titus 1:4	The altar of sacrifice	Conversion / repentance
Little faith	Matthew 8:26	The laver	Separation
Temporary faith	Luke 8:13	The table of shewbread	Study of the word of God and fellowship

Strong faith	Romans 4:18-22	The candlestick	Testimony
Creative faith	Matthew 8:10	The incense altar	Prayer
Active faith	James 1:22-25	The Ark of the Covenant	Full surrender
Divine faith	Galatians 3:22	The mercy seat	Victory – The anointing

Allow me to give you my definition of faith. This was given to me in 1979 in a Bible study group and I never forgot it. It goes like this: *"Faith, because of trust, is that **quality**, not **quantity**, of **power** whereby the things **hoped** for become the things **possessed**"*

WHERE ARE YOU ON THE LADDER?

Using this definition, ask yourself three questions: Where are you on the ladder? Are you going *up* or *down* the ladder? Where do you want to be? Only you know the answers to these questions; but where you are on the ladder determines where you are *"in Yeshua"* according to you, not God.

What is God's goal for your life? There are people who will go through what I call, the "whosoever gate." They will place their lives at the altar of sacrifice, then turn and leave, praising God. They have missed the goal. The goal is the Holy of Holies.

Then there are people who, after going through the "whosoever gate" and the altar of sacrifice, continue to the laver where they are washed with the baptism of repentance as done by John. Again, they will turn and leave, praising God. These people see God as the prophet, but not as the priest or king, and they have missed the goal. The goal is the Holy of Holies.

There are people who want more of God. These people will go through the "whosoever gate," and, after laying down their lives at the altar of sacrifice, and being cleansed at the laver, will enter into the Holy Place. Once inside, they will fellowship with other believers around the table of shewbread. They will then leave praising God, but would have missed the goal. The goal is the Holy of Holies.

Fewer people will go through the "whosoever gate," through the courtyard with the altar of sacrifice and laver, then into the Holy Place. After the fellowship with other believers at the table of shewbread, they will go to the menorah for in-depth Scripture study. They will then, praising God, turn and leave. They also have missed the goal. The goal is the Holy of Holies.

Again, even fewer people will go through the same process and will continue to the altar of incense. It is here that they will enter into intercessory prayer. These people in the Holy Place see God as the prophet and priest, but not as their king. When finished, they will turn and leave, believing they have met with God. They may have, but they missed the goal, which is the Holy of Holies.

Even less people will go through the same process and will continue past the altar of incense, and through the veil. They can now see the Ark of the Covenant. They see God as the prophet, priest, and their king. They recognize the authority of God, and it changes their thought patterns and their lives. They leave, praising God, accepting His kingship, and changing their lives forever. They made it into the Holy of Holies, but still missed the goal: the mercy seat.

The Scripture says, *"Many are called, but few are chosen"* (Matthew 22:14 KJV). Who are the chosen? They are simply those who choose to go. There is that blessed person who goes through the "whosoever gate," lays down his life at the altar of sacrifice, goes to the laver, separating himself from his past life, and goes into the Holy Place. There, he fellowships with other believers around the table of shewbread, goes into in-depth study of God's word at the menorah, and enter into intercessory prayer at the altar of incense.

He will go past the veil, and, by recognizing the authority of God in his life, change the lifestyle of his walk. He will stand before the mercy seat of the Ark of the Covenant. He now experiences the presence of God on his life. Once there, he will not want to leave. He has reached the goal: the mercy seat of the Holy of Holies, where the presence of God is located.

The Scriptures say, in Romans 12:1-2, these words:

"I beseech you therefore, brethren, by the mercies of God, that ye present your bodies a living sacrifice, holy, acceptable unto God, which is your reasonable service. And be not conformed to this world: but be ye transformed by the renewing of your mind, that ye may prove what is that **good, and acceptable, and perfect, will of God** [emphasis mine]."

The "good will of God" is seen in the courtyard and as the prophet. The "acceptable (or well-pleasing) will of God" is seen in the Holy Place as the priest. The "perfect will of God" is seen in the Holy of Holies, as the king.

WHAT IS YOUR LIGHT SOURCE?

You walk in the light you have. If you have **common faith** and move to **little faith,** the light comes from the courtyard. This is the light of creation, which is the sun, moon, and stars – the lights of nature. The light of nature on the outside of the tabernacle is the light of human reason, philosophy, and speculation.

A man who follows reason instead of faith can reject the Word of God. Instead of faith and trust, he substitutes reason and philosophy. Instead of the blood, he substitutes religion, morality, ethics, ordinances, education, psychology, and psychiatry. On this, read: *"But a natural man does not accept the things of the Spirit of God, for they are foolishness to him, and he cannot understand them, for they are spiritually appraised"* (1 Corinthians 2:14 ASV).

When you move into **temporary faith**, through **strong faith**, to **creative faith**, you have a greater sense of God's presence on your life. Your light comes from the light of the menorah reflecting off the golden walls of the tabernacle in the Holy Place. It covers the entire Holy Place with a sense of God's presence.

If your faith connects to God's holy presence and moves to **active faith,** then **divine faith**, you have walked into the Holy of Holies. The only light in this place is God's *Shchinah* glory. You have reached the level where you can move in the power of the *Ruach Hakodesh*. You are on your Mount of Transfiguration and your life will never be the same. (See Appendix 2)

THE DECISION

"See, I have set before thee this day life and good, and death and evil; In that I command thee this day to love the LORD thy God, to walk in his ways, and to keep his commandments and his statutes and his judgments, that thou mayest live and multiply: and the LORD thy God shall bless thee in the land whither thou goest to possess it. But if thine heart turn away, so that thou wilt not hear, but shalt be drawn away, and worship other gods, and serve them; I denounce unto you this day, that ye shall surely perish, and that ye shall not prolong your days upon the land, whither thou passest over Jordan to go to possess it."

"I call heaven and earth to record this day against you, that I have set before you life and death, blessing and cursing: therefore choose life, that both thou and thy seed may live: That thou mayest love the LORD thy God, and that thou mayest obey his voice, and that thou mayest cleave unto him: for he is thy life, and the length of thy days: that thou mayest dwell in the land which the LORD sware unto thy fathers, to Abraham, to Isaac, and to Jacob, to give them" (Deuteronomy 30:15-20 KJV).

In a sporting event, the referee would take a coin; flip it into the air, and call, "heads or tails?" The winner would be able to make favorable decisions. I would, at all times, choose heads, and never tails. I wanted to be the head, never the tail. Israel had to choose between heads or tails, and so must you.

When Moses said these words, he was one hundred twenty years old, and, according to Jewish tradition, this was the last day of his life. "This day" is recorded in verses 2, 8, 15, 16, 18, 19. He is not repeating himself to be heard, but emphasizing it. This is Moses' last shot. There is finality in the message, laying a foundation. Moses is now *"flipping the coin"* for you. What will be your choice?

There is no fence. You cannot sit and ponder your choice. Moses laid down the gauntlet of God: choose life or choose death. It demands a decision. A non-decision is a wrong decision. Why? There is no such thing as a non-choice! A non-choice is rejection of God!

Choice requires cost. For every choice you make, there is a cost to be paid, either good or bad. You have the freedom to take which course you choose, but you do not have the freedom to determine the end of that choice. God makes clear what he desires. You must choose. *"Choose life, that you may live"* (Deuteronomy 30:19 KJV).

Consider this point in history: A man named George Wilson was tried and convicted to die for a murder committed in 1829. His friends prevailed upon President Andrew Jackson to issue a pardon for him. President Jackson issued the pardon. What did Wilson do? He refused it!

The case went all the way to the Supreme Court, which made a final judgment. The nine judges ruled that a pardon is no good unless accepted by the person for whom it was issued. George Wilson died while having a Presidential pardon sitting on the sheriff's desk. Is there anyone you know who has a *"pardon"* sitting on the desk of God, and who has refused it, either outright or by sitting on the fence?

If You Are Jewish

One of the names for the Feast of Rosh Hashanah is called the "Day of the Blowing of the Shofar." Do you know how the Shofar is made?

In Psalm 150:3-6, it reads:

"Praise Him with the sound on the shofar! Praise Him with lute and lyre! Praise Him with tambourines and dancing! Praise Him with flutes and strings! Praise Him with clanging cymbals! Let everything that has breath praise Adonai! Halleluyah!" (CJB).

I want to call your attention to two observations: the first observation is that out of all the worship tools listed in this psalm, the first mentioned is the shofar. Before the stringed instruments, before the wind instruments, and before the tambourines and dance, the shofar is distinguished as being one of the most important worship tools available to you. For that reason, Scripture authorizes its use in the worship service.

The second observation is found in verse 6. *"Let everything that has breath praise Adonai."* For you to understand this verse and how it is related to the shofar, it must be known what must be done to the shofar before it can be blown.

To begin with, unlike the stringed or brass instruments, the shofar is not man-made. It is a natural instrument, composed of flesh, blood, and bone, with the bone being the shofar, itself. It is also the only worship tool created by God. No man can claim to have created it. Only God has that distinction. Before the shofar can become an instrument of praise, the flesh has to be removed. When the shofar is removed from a ram, the first thing that must be done is to extract the flesh and blood from the inside of the shofar. This process does not always remove all of the flesh from the inside, accounting for the familiar, unpleasant odor when not done correctly.

After the shofar is cleaned thoroughly in the inside, the next step is to remove the rough edges from the outside. The shofar is sanded and polished to bring out the natural beauty of the shofar. This process, by intense friction, removes the Shofar's callous and rugged exterior.

The next process is to form and reshape the shofar to produce the sound that you are accustomed to hearing. To do this, the shofar must be softened by intense heat and pressure. When the heat has brought the shofar to its desired pliability, the craftsman can reshape the instrument as he sees fit.

The last process is the most important. The shofar is pierced at the smaller end. This creates a place through which air can pass, creating the sound, or voice, of the Shofar.

Every procedure in the creation of the shofar culminates with this: breath being blown through an object, which before was crude and inanimate, transforming it into an instrument of praise to the Almighty. Even with all the preparation and work that goes into the creation of the shofar, if breath does not pass through the shofar, it fails to serve its purpose.

You are like the shofar. We have been created for a purpose, which is to praise Adonai.

In order to become an instrument of praise, you must allow the Master Craftsman to remove the flesh from your life. The Scripture says, *"They that worship Him must worship Him in spirit and in truth"* (John 4:24 KJV). If the flesh is not removed in worship, then just like the shofar defect, the odor goes into the nostrils of God and it is not a *"sweet savor"* (Leviticus 17:6 KJV).

Then you must allow the Master Craftsman to remove the rough edges and polish you into a beautiful instrument.

God allows trials and tribulations to come your way in order to produce the heat and pressure need to mode you into the instrument He wants you to be. In the last process, you must be willing to allow God to pierce your hearts so you will be opened and prepared for His breath: His *Ruach Hakodesh.*

When God breathes His Spirit into you, you will become the instrument of praise you were created to be.

Another name for Rosh Hashanah is called the "Day of Judgment."

In the Jewish Rosh Hashanah prayers you say: *"You have remembered us unto life, and you have written us into the Book of Life, for Your sake, O God of Life."*[56] To honestly pray this prayer and ask God for life, you must first make the decision to choose life.

If you attended Hebrew school as a young child, then you have an advantage over most people. Let's look at an example: When the Torah is returned to the ark during the service on Shabbat these words are said:

"Ha-she-vay-noo Adonai, ay-leh-cha v'na-shoo-va, Chadash ya-may-noo k'keh-dem." In English it reads: *"Bring us back Lord to You, and we shall come. Renew our days as of old"*[57]

Because of your knowledge of Hebrew, you know when a Hebrew word like "chadash", which means, "renew," is mistranslated or applied in a different way (See Appendix 4). You also know when it is applied rightly and within its context. Now, apply your knowledge to the chapter of scripture that is bypassed and never read in your synagogue: Isaiah 53

Rashi was the first Rabbi to interpret the suffering servant of Isaiah 53 as Israel. This was a thousand years after the destruction of the temple. Before the idea of Rashi existed in the mind of his great-great grandmother, the ancient sages always taught that Isaiah 53 applied to the Messiah.

There is no single ancient Jewish reference, not the Babylonian and Jerusalem Talmuds, the Targums, or the midrashim, stating that Isaiah 53 was ever applied to Israel as the whole nation for over the first thousand years from the Second Temple period.

Even in our day, some Rabbis interpret Isaiah 53 to an individual Messiah, and not to the nation of Israel as a whole. If this was not true, how could followers of the ultra-orthodox Lubavitcher Rebbe Schneerson, in our day interpret Isaiah 53, and apply it to their leader who lived and died two thousand five hundred years after the return from the Babylonian exile?

The collection of Midrashim came together the same time as the Talmud. They both finished at about the same time, which was around 550 C.E. The church's "renewed covenant" scriptures were codified in 397 C.E. There is over one hundred years between the two.

I am going to ask you a hard question. With all the major problems that existed between Christianity and Judaism during that period, and the fact that the church, claiming to be the "*New Israel,*" was using Isaiah 53 to proclaim Jesus as their Jewish Messiah, why is there not a single Midrash backing Rashi's position?

You cannot answer this question from silence. It is the Rabbi's position to protect his students.

If Rashi's position were correct, there would have been at least one Midrash supporting Rashi's position during that time.

Here is another point to consider:

Isaiah 53:4-6 reads: "*Surely He has borne our griefs and carried our sorrows; but He was wounded for our transgressions. He was bruised for our iniquities; the chastisement for our peace was upon Him, and with His stripes we are healed. All we like sheep have gone astray; we have turned, everyone, to his own way; and the Lord has laid on Him the iniquity of us all*" (KJV).

With these verses in mind, consider reading an ancient "*musaf*" prayer for Yom Kippur. This prayer did exist, but is no longer found in the Day of Atonement liturgy, nor is it usually read in the modern observance of the feast:

"*Our righteous Anointed (The Messiah) is departed from us: Horror hath seized us, and we have none to justify us. He has borne the yoke of our iniquities and our transgressions, and is wounded because of our transgression. He bears our sins on His shoulder, that we may find pardon for our iniquities.*

We shall be healed by His wound, at the time that the Eternal will create Him [The Messiah] as a new creature"
[58]

The writer of this ancient prayer understood the words spoken concerning the Messiah by the Hebrew prophet, Isaiah. It has special meaning to those who believe Yeshua is the suffering servant.

Even though sacrificing continued until the temple was destroyed, sacrifices were to no avail as regarding the forgiveness of sins according to the Talmud. (Yoma 39b) That is the reason God permitted the temple and all the records of the priesthood genealogies to be destroyed.

This is the first time since the inception of Judaism that there is no record as to who the priests are. The reason is because the priesthood is no longer of any value.

"*For the life of the flesh is in the blood; and I have given it to you upon the altar to make an atonement for your souls; for it is the blood that maketh an atonement for the soul,*"

(Leviticus 17:11). Without the shedding of blood, there is no remission of sin.

You are unclean before God. This is not because the temple was destroyed and you can no longer sacrifice, but because you have not accepted the sacrifice of God's only Son. He is the one who paid the price God demanded to abolish your sin.

Even if you think you are a good person, you have no protection. That is because you have no covering for your sins and because your sins have not been paid for. In God's eyes, you are wicked.

God says in Ezekiel 33:11, "*Say unto them, As I live saith the Lord God, I have no pleasure in the death of the wicked, but that the wicked turn from his way and live; turn ye, turn ye from your evil ways; for why will you die, O house of Israel?*" (KJV)

"*Turn ye unto me, saith the Lord of Hosts and I will turn unto you*" (Zechariah 1:3 KJV).

In the United States, you can be wrong about God, and nothing, by US Law, will happen to you. But God never gives you the right to be wrong, especially about Him.

Being Jewish, you have accepted the covenant of Moses, but you will stand before God under the covenant with fear. Why? God will demand judgment under the covenant of Moses, alone; but if you also accept the renewed covenant under Yeshua, you do not stand before God with fear. Why? The judgment required by the covenant of Moses was satisfied under the renewed covenant of Yeshua.

If You Are Gentile

In all of Paul's writings, the word "*justification,*" when applied to the Gentile is used over eighty times; but the word "*repentance,*" when applied to Gentiles, was never used. The word "*repentance*" is only applied to the Jewish people. WHY? At the point of salvation, the word "*repentance*" implies a *"returning to where you came from,"* which would, when applied to the Gentile, require them to go back to idol worship. It is after salvation and living the life of a new man that repentance comes into play.

If you are a Gentile with the heart of Ruth, and the spirit of Caleb, you have also accepted the covenant of Moses, but you have the same problem as a Jewish person. You will find yourself standing before God under the covenant with fear for the same reason.

If you also accept the renewed covenant under the Lordship of Yeshua, that fear is gone replaced by joy. Consider this: Three things must be completed to become part of the covenant of Moses: the circumcision, the *T'zilah* (water baptism), and the sacrifice.

If you are under the renewed covenant, then through Yeshua, you have fulfilled these requirements in Colossians 2 and had your certificate of debt nailed to the execution stake. You have been brought into the Commonwealth of Israel, and can stand before God with trust and love under the Jewish olive tree recorded in Romans 9-11, as explained in another chapter.

If you are not under the renewed covenant, then you are a pagan. This also has been discussed in another chapter, but this scripture is designed to remind you: *"It is a terrifying thing to fall into the hands of the living God"* (Hebrews 10:31 ASV).

Your Level Of Fear

Both of you, Jew and Gentile, were taught that fear is bad. For example, you are only scared of fire when you think it might harm you. Once you know how to respect and relate to fire properly, there is nothing to fear.

However, it is the fear of fire's danger that helps keep you in right relationship with it. It's the same with God. You don't have to be scared of him unless you are not in right relationship with Him.

Scriptures teaches you that sometimes God's methods of revelation are chosen to produce fear. This type of fear does not go away, and yet, produces the fruit of peace. Fearing God means knowing who you are and who He is. This places what He says over what you feel or wish He had said. He has been given a priority in your life. Some people understand the fear of God as meaning, *"being afraid of God."* There is an element of being afraid of God, but this level of fear exists in a different realm.

Being afraid would, in the flesh, cause you to distance yourself from the object of that fear, but this fear of God does the opposite. It moves you closer to Him. This fear of God exists within the confines of a covenant relationship, one in which the greater the fear, the greater the relationship.

Instead of separating, the fear of God draws you closer to the One who is to be worshipped. Yet, by drawing closer, the realization of His greatness and holiness increases, and your respect and love grows stronger and greater.

As you live your life in the growing and maturing fear of God, you find your life living in accordance with His righteousness. This brings home the reality of Solomon's conclusion in the book of Ecclesiastes.

"Let us hear the conclusion of the whole matter: Fear God, and keep his commandments: for this is the whole duty of man" (Ecclesiastes 12:13 KJV).

C.S. Lewis once said, *"When the author walks onto the stage, the play is over. God is going to invade, all right; but what is the good of saying you are on His side then, when you see the whole natural universe melting away like a dream and something else comes crashing in?"*

At this time, it will be God without disguise; something so overwhelming that it will strike either irresistible love, or irresistible horror into every creature. It will be too late then to choose your side.

That will not be the time for choosing; It will be the time when you discover which side you really have chosen, whether you realized it before or not. Now, today, this moment is your chance to choose the right side.

Both of you, Jew and Gentile, are on the crossroads to eternity. Your choice will determine your destiny. "Now *choose life, so that you and your children may live*" (Deuteronomy 30:19 NIV). The coin is being flipped; what is your choice: heads or tails?

IX   THE CALL OF GOD ON YOUR LIFE

"No person was ever honored for what he received. Honor has been the reward for what he gave."

Calvin Coolidge (1872 – 1933)

IX. THE CALL OF GOD ON YOUR LIFE

—⟨ɷɷ⟩—

> *"Brothers, I, for my part, do not think of myself as having yet gotten hold of it; but one thing I do: forgetting what is behind me and straining forward toward what lies ahead, I keep pursuing the goal in order to win the prize offered by God's upward calling in the Messiah Yeshua."* (Philippians 3:13-14 CJB)

WHAT IS YOUR EXCUSE?

Have you ever felt confused about God's calling on your life? Many have, and like Moses, they thought by taking things into their own hands they could accomplish the will of God. God's will consists of three things: His Name, His Word, and His Kingdom.

When you accepted Yeshua as your Savior, Lord, and King, you became a citizen in the kingdom of God. You were not placed there to be a *pew-warmer* or to receive *fire insurance* from hell. You were placed in God's kingdom to be a warrior: to honor His name, spread His Word, and advance the kingdom of God on the earth.

You have no reason to reject this position, and mission, so my next question is, what is your excuse? Do you offer the same excuses that Moses did when God called him to lead the children of Israel out of bondage from Egypt into the Promised Land? Let's look at the call of Moses.

THE CALL OF MOSES

Before Moses was given his calling, God trained and educated him for his preparation. According to scriptures, Moses received his education from two universities. The first forty years, Moses was a student, a statesman, and a soldier in the courts of Egypt.

As a student, "*And Moses was instructed in all the wisdom of the Egyptians; and he was mighty in his words and works*" (Acts 7:22 ASV). As a statesman, he learned the procedures used at the throne of Pharaoh. As a soldier Jewish tradition states that when the Phoenicians attacked Egypt, Moses led the Egyptian army and completely routed them.

The second forty years was as a shepherd in the wilderness.

"*Now Moses was keeping the flock of Jethro his father-in-law, the priest of Midian: and he led the flock to the back of the wilderness, and came to the mountain of God, unto Horeb*" (Exodus 3:1 ASV).

It took forty years as a shepherd, on the backside of the desert, to remove the teachings from Egypt that would not be profitable for his calling. In addition, Moses needed, in ability to answer his calling, these three things.

- He needed to know how to rule, because he was to become a leader of millions.
- He needed military training, because he had to be a strategist and fight wars.
- He needed to be able to read and write to record the history of the Torah and all its teachings.

All of the different stages of Moses' life were necessary to equip him for his calling. You will go through this same process. God will prepare and train you for your calling.

"Such is the confidence we have through the Messiah toward God. It is not that we are competent in ourselves to count anything as having come from us; on the contrary, our competence is from God. He has even made us competent to be workers serving a New Covenant, the essence of which is not a written text but the Spirit. For the written text brings death, but the Spirit gives life" (2 Corinthians 3:4-6 CJB).

MOSES' OPERATING IN THE CALLING

There are three lessons you can learn as you study the call of Moses. These lessons are that it requires preparation, that it requires the knowledge of God, and, last, that it requires total surrender.

The first lesson you can learn from the call of Moses is that it requires preparation.

God allowed Moses to go through the wilderness experience for forty years. Moses had no idea when his life experience went from future king to shepherd that God was preparing him to shepherd His people out of slavery. His wilderness experience was not a waste of time and talent, but for training and preparation. This is where Moses learned isolation. Moses was eighty years old when he answered the call of God. What does that mean to you? It says you are never too old for God to use you.

The person qualified may not be called, but the person God calls, He qualifies. Look at your wilderness experience in the same way. To listen to the voice of God, you must be alone with God. The distractions of the world will drown out the voice of God.

The second lesson learned from the call of Moses is that it required the knowledge of God.

Sometimes God will appear in the most unlikely place or time and fill you with a sense of His presence and power. Has this ever happened to you?

Moses was not looking for God when God made Himself known. God came to him while he was doing what he did for forty years, shepherding the flock of Jethro. Moses first experienced God's presence and power at the burning bush. If you are going to move in your calling, you will also experience your burning bush. What is your burning bush?

With this experience, Moses started to understand the knowledge of God. What was that knowledge?

God Is Holy

The first piece of knowledge Moses had of God was that God is Holy. God told him to remove his sandals from his feet because he was standing on holy ground. When you answer God's call, this will also be your first piece of knowledge of God. When you recognize the holiness and authority of God, pride will not enter your calling. God's holiness and authority will cause you to continue to come before Him to confess your sins and ask for forgiveness.

God Is Faithful

God called Moses by name and reminded him there was a history of God's faithfulness with Moses' ancestors. He told Moses He was God to Moses' fathers – the God of Abraham, the God of Isaac, and the God of Jacob. From the normal process of your daily life, God calls you by name.

When that happens, take off the *shoes of your heart*. You are on holy ground, made holy by the God of your ancestors. In times of difficulty, you can count on God's presence and help. When you hear Him call your name, this assurance can allow you to say with your entire being, "Here I Am."

God Is Compassionate

"Sometime during those many years the king of Egypt died, but the people of Isra'el still groaned under the yoke of slavery, and they cried out, and their cry for rescue from slavery came up to God. God heard their groaning, and God remembered his covenant with Avraham, Yitz'chak and Ya'akov. God saw the people of Isra'el, and God acknowledged them" (Exodus 2:23-25 CJB).

God was concerned and moved by the Israelites' misery, and told Moses. This perfect love triangle – Moses, God, and the people of Israel – became the template for the remainder of Moses' life. The book of Exodus is an interweaving of the three different points of this love triangle. Whatever purpose God has prepared for your life, like Moses, He will fulfill. He will draw you into this same triangle.

GOD'S THREE GOALS FOR YOU

God's purpose for you will accomplish three goals at once. Your calling throws light on who you are. It brings fulfillment to the passion and potential God has invested in your personality. The call of God gives you the ultimate expression to your identity.

Second, your calling releases you to be who you were created to be. It will move you towards the meeting of the needs of those on whom the love of God is focused. The authenticity of your calling is this acid test. Connection with God did not disconnect Moses from the needs of the world. It took him deeper in; so will it be with you.

Last, your calling is an expression of who God is. The character of God produces the call of God. It contributes to the fulfillment of God's purposes for the earth.

On the field of battle, you only see the campaigns in which you fight. God sees the whole war. He lets you know your small acts have significance on the global scale.

GOD'S PLAN OF ACTION

"I have come down to rescue them from the Egyptians and to bring them up out of that country to a good and spacious land, a land flowing with milk and honey, the place of the Kena'ani, Hitti, Emori, P'rizi, Hivi and Y'vusi. Yes, the cry of the people of Isra'el has come to me, and I have seen how terribly the Egyptians oppress them. Therefore, now, come; and I will send you to Pharaoh; so that you can lead my people, the descendants of Isra'el, out of Egypt" (Exodus 3:8-10 CJB).

God's plan was to rescue His people and take them into a special land. Likewise, God has a special plan for you. Feeding the poor, playing sports, helping with special events, cooking, shopping for old people, campaigning for justice, engaging in party political affairs, creating and using wealth, writing, teaching, recording, all of these - and more - can and do have a place in God's purpose.

These normal acts are transformed into God's mission when they are in response to His word, and in obedience to the prompting of the *Ruach Hakodesh*. Now you know why the knowledge of God is essential. If you receive a call from Him without knowing Him, how can, or do, you respond?

THE FIVE EXCUSES

Excuses, excuses, excuses! You make them when you wonder if you are up to the task that you were asked or called to do, especially if it is God giving you the call. You are no different from Moses in that respect.

The third lesson learned from the call of Moses is it requires total surrender. Moses resisted the call.

He thought he had none of the skills required for the job that God set before him. He gave God five excuses why he could not perform His command. In each case, God answered his excuses. God reassured Moses repeatedly. Look at the excuses of Moses, and see how God's word answers them for you.

"I Have No Ability" (Exodus 3:11)

The first words Moses spoke to God were, "Here am I." Now he says, "Who am I?" This first excuse could be called, *"crossed-eyed theology."* Moses forgot who was the deliverer. Exodus 3:7-10 reads, *"The Lord said, 'I [emphasis mine] have indeed seen the misery of my people in Egypt. I [emphasis mine] have heard them crying out because of their slave drivers, and I [emphasis mine] am concerned about their suffering."*

"So I [emphasis mine] have come down to rescue them from the hand of the Egyptians and to bring them up out of that land into a good and spacious land, a land flowing with milk and honey—the home of the Canaanites, Hittites, Amorites, Perizzites, Hivites and Jebusites."

"And now, the cry of the Israelites has reached me, and I [emphasis mine] have seen the way the Egyptians are oppressing them."

"So now, go. I [emphasis mine] am sending you to Pharaoh to bring my people the Israelites out of Egypt'" *(NIV).*

Moses was not the deliverer. God wanted to deliver the children of Israel through Moses. Readiness has turned into reluctance when Moses understood the mission. In Judges 6:15, Gideon has a similar objection. As with Moses, God's answer was also reassurance. He promised to be with him, and that was enough for Gideon, but not Moses. Are you a "Gideon" or a "Moses?"

Moses had the perfect example of what God wanted to do with him: the burning bush. The burning bush was an ordinary bush, which became extraordinary by the power that was in the bush. You also can become God's "burning bush," if you operate in the calling God placed on your life.

Are you going to accept His calling, or will you offer excuses? Can you use this excuse? What is God's answer to you when you apply it?

"and, lo, I am with you always, even unto the end of the world. Amen" (Matthew 28:20 KJV). This is added to your command to go.

"If God is for us, who can be against us?" (Romans 8:31 KJV)

"I can do all things through him who gives me power" (Philippians 4:13 CJB).

"I Have No Message" (Exodus 3:13)

Moses now says, *"What if the Israelites ask who sent me?"* Moses is asking, *"Who are You, God? What is Your Name?"* This excuse can be called, *"hiding behind insufficient knowledge."* How did God answer Moses? In today's language, He would have said, *"Moses, it is not what you know, it is whom you know."* God identifies Himself to Moses as the same God whom the patriarchs worshiped. God is not a new God, but the God who has already acted on behalf of Israel. There is no higher authority. God's answer in Hebrew was *"Ehyeh Aser Ehyeh"*.

This can be translated a number of ways:

- I Am Who I Am
- I Will Be What (Who) I Will Be
- I Will Cause To Be What I Will Cause To Be
- I Will Be Who I Am
- I Am Who I Will Be
- I Will Be With You Wherever You Go

According to ancient Hebrew thought, knowledge of the name gave some degree of control over the person. When God gave His name, He showed His willingness to be called on. The name does not confine or explain God. He is still beyond our comprehension and we cannot control Him.

When you offer this excuse, what does the Word of God say about your message?

"For among the first things I passed on to you was what I also received, namely this: the Messiah died for our sins, in accordance with what the Tanakh says;"

"and he was buried; and he was raised on the third day, in accordance with what the Tanakh says" (1 Corinthians 15:3-4 CJB).

It is not what you know, but whom you know that counts.

"I Have No Authority" (Exodus 4:1-9)

In this third excuse, Moses shows his doubt in God's ability. In Exodus 3:18, God said this to Moses:

*"**They will heed what you say** [emphasis mine]. Then you will come, you and the leaders of Isra'el, before the king of Egypt; and you will tell him, 'ADONAI, the God of the Hebrews, has met with us. Now, please, let us go three days' journey into the desert; so that we can sacrifice to ADONAI our God'"* (CJB).

Does Moses believe God? No. Moses shows his unbelief in Exodus 4:1.

"Moshe replied, 'But I'm certain they won't believe me, and they won't listen to what I say, because they'll say, 'ADONAI did not appear to you'" (CJB).

God does not take offense. He takes the question seriously and gives additional resources. Moses is given three signs to convince the people that it is God doing the deliverance.

The first sign, changing the staff into a snake, showed God's ability to influence the inanimate and animal world. By changing the nature of an inanimate object, the staff, God influenced Moses' behavior.

The Torah reports Moses fled from the snake. God tells Moses to pick up his staff – by its tail. Who picks up a snake by its tail? Moses trusted God and did it. From that point on, the staff became Moses' symbol of God's power within his calling.

The second sign, inflicting Moses with leprosy than healing him, showed God's influence on the human body.

The third sign, changing water into blood, showed God's power over the essence of human life: water and blood. Both the spiritual side of man, symbolized by the water, and the physical side of man, represented by the blood, are under God's influence.

What does God give you to help others believe the message you bring? Spiritual gifts!

"Now concerning spiritual gifts, brethren, I would not have you ignorant... But all these worketh that one and the selfsame Spirit, dividing to every man severally as he will" (1 Corinthians 12: 1, 11 KJV).

"I have No Eloquence" (Exodus 4:10-12)

Moses' fourth excuse was a lack of *word power*. He uses his disability in an attempt to back out. God will not let it drop. He reminds Moses that He made him, and will put the words in his mouth.

Can you use this excuse in an attempt to back out of the calling God placed on your life? Not if you believe the Word of God. Scripture will not allow it. In 1 Corinthians 2:12-13, it says:

"Now we have received, not the spirit of the world, but the spirit, which is of God; that we might know the things that are freely given to us of God. Which things also we speak, not in the words which man's wisdom teacheth, but which the <u>Ruach Hakodesh</u> [my translation] teacheth; comparing spiritual things with spiritual" (KJV).

"I Have No Inclination" (Exodus 4:13-17)

Moses' last excuse was, *"Please pick someone else!"* As long as Moses' reasons were his own shortcomings, God responded with a clear and precise rebuttal, but when Moses said, *"Oh, Lord, please send someone else,"* without offering any reason on his shortcomings, He was showing a lack of trust, and trying to shift responsibility.

God got angry, and went to *"Plan B."* In today's language, God said, *"Moses, this is not a request. I am telling you – Go!"* Aaron would be Moses' speaker. Moses had to learn to surrender himself to God and trust in His guidance.

Can you use this excuse? How does God answer this excuse in your life and calling?

"For it is God who worketh in you both to will and to work, for his good pleasure. Do all things without murmurings and questionings: that ye may become blameless and harmless, children of God without blemish in the midst of a crooked and perverse generation, among whom ye are seen as lights in the world" (Philippians 2:13-15 ASV).

When challenged with the difficult tasks of your calling, you must face the mission and challenge presented to you, and deal with your own abilities. By shifting the responsibility to someone else, even if you feel they are better qualified, you may be inviting anger. Why?

When God asks you to perform, there is no one better qualified to do His mission. He has a vested interest in you. Do not ignore God's calling. You need to let God prepare you, increase in knowledge of Him, and surrender yourself fully to Him.

The fourth and last lesson Moses learned about his calling was accountability. Because of his anger, which he thought was under control, he was not able to enter into the Promised Land, but this is not the end of the story.

The *Brit Hadashah* tells the story of the Mountain of Transfiguration in Israel where Moses replaced his goal from the Promised Land to the Promised One.

You are also accountable for your calling. Scripture says: *"From everyone who has been given much, much will be required; and to whom they entrusted much, of him they will ask all the more"* (Luke 12:48 ASV).

Matthew 25:14-30 tells the story about the parable of the talents. The third servant did not hear the words, *"Well done, thou good and faithful servant."* He took the talent God had given him to use and buried it. What were the words he heard? Verse 30 reads *"Throw out the unprofitable servant into the outer darkness, where there will be weeping and gnashing of teeth."* He did not enter into the joy of the kingdom. Do not make the same mistake.

CONCLUSION

Let this be the battle cry of your calling:

"Brothers, I, for my part, do not think of myself as having yet gotten hold of it; but one thing I do: forgetting what is behind me and straining forward toward what lies ahead, I keep pursuing the goal in order to win the prize offered by God's upward calling in the Messiah Yeshua" (Philippians 3:13-14 CJB).

Re-read the words of Isaiah 1:18:

*"Come Now, and let us **reason together** [emphasis mine]," saith the Lord: "Though your sins be as Scarlet, they **shall be** [emphasis mine] as white as snow; though they be red like crimson, they shall be as wool"* (KJV).

God has always had a man or woman He raised up to follow His calling. When the children of Israel needed to be delivered, He raised up Moses. When the spies gave a bad report, He raised up Joshua and Caleb. When their enemies attacked the children of Israel, God intervened. He raised up twelve men and one woman called judges. When the priesthood was corrupt, He raised up Samuel. When the monarchy was in rebellion, He anointed David. When the nation practiced idol worship, He raised up Elijah. When Haman tried to destroy the Jewish people, Esther accepted God's call. Ezra answered the call to bring Israel back from captivity. When Jerusalem's walls were broken down, God called Nehemiah to rebuild them.

God has always had a man or woman to answer His call. Are you willing to be God's called person for this generation? Will you answer His call or will you give excuses?

This book started with the Word of God recorded in Isaiah 28:9-10. I would like to sum up the context of this book with another Scripture. It is recorded in 1 Corinthians 3:9-15.

"For we are God's fellow-workers: you are God's field, God's building. By the grace God has given me, I laid a foundation as an expert builder; and someone else is building on it; but each one should be careful how he builds.

"For no one can lay any foundation other than the one already laid, which is <u>Yeshua, the Messiah</u> [my translation]."

"If any man builds on this foundation using gold, silver, costly stones, wood, hay, straw; his work will be shown for what it is: because the Day will bring it to light. It will be revealed with fire; and the fire will test the quality of each man's work."

"If what he builds survives, he will receive his reward. If it is burned up, he will suffer loss; he himself will be saved; but only as one escaping through the flames" (NIV).

X APPENDIXES

1) The "Baptism" Of The Ruach Hakodesh
2) The Power Of Psalm 91
3) Paul's Double Concept Of The "Law"
4) The Word "New"
5) Yeshua, The Living Torah

APPENDIXES

—⚜—

Appendix 1 - The Baptism Of The *Ruach*

Hakodesh

There have been more debates and divisions in the body of Messiah over these six words, "the Baptism of the *Ruach Hakodesh* [Holy Spirit]," than any other doctrine. Interpretations differ as to what the "Baptism of the *Ruach Hakodesh*" means to the believer's experience. The purpose of this book is not to add to the debates and divisions, but to furnish a Hebraic and historical understanding.

The word "*baptism*" is not a translation. It is a transliteration. What that means is they take the Greek word, twist it a little bit, and make it into an English word instead if translating it.

Let me give you another example. The word "*adelphos*" means "brother." When it is transliterated, it would say "*adelpho*" or one of its variants. The translator would, by twisting it and applying it within its context make it mean "brother." The word "baptize" is done in the same way.

The Greek word *"baptizo"* is only adjusted for the English Language. You don't really know what it means, so you must learn it somewhere else.

The word *"baptizo"* is a word used in the ancient dye and garment industry. If you took a white shirt and dunked it into red dye, the white shirt would become red, soaked with the red dye. The white shirt has taken on the properties and characteristics of the red dye. The action of plunging and bringing out was called *"baptizo."*

When you are baptized, there is the picture of being dipped into water. When it comes to the phase, "baptism of the *Ruach Hakodesh*," it is not just the picture of going under and coming up. It is the picture of the soaking up the dye. You are immersed in the Spirit and the Spirit is immersed in you. You are soaked with the Spirit, and you are changed, just like the white shirt when it is dipped in the red dye.

"For in one Spirit were we all baptized into one body, whether Jews or Greeks, whether bond or free; and were all made to drink of one Spirit" (1 Corinthians 12:13 KJV).

This is the picture of you being dunked into the *Ruach Hakodesh*, soaking up the *Ruach Hakodesh*, and becoming one with the *Ruach Hakodesh*.

A Hebraic and historical understanding of the *"baptism of the Ruach Hakodesh"* does not start at Acts 2. Did you know that in Acts 2, God was not doing a *"new thing?"* To understand, you must begin your walk in the Torah with Numbers 11.

"The Lord said to Moses: 'Bring me seventy of Israel's elders who are known to you as leaders and officials among the people. Have them come to the Tent of Meeting, that they may stand there with you. I will come down and speak with you there, and I will take of the Spirit that is on you and put the Spirit on them. They will help you carry the burden of the people so that you will not have to carry it alone'" (Numbers 11:16-17 NIV).

"So Moses went out and told the people what the Lord had said. He brought together seventy of their elders and had them stand around the Tent. Then the Lord came down in the cloud and spoke with him, and he took of the Spirit that was on him and put the Spirit on the seventy elders. When the Spirit rested on them, they prophesied, but they did not do so again. However, two men, whose names were Eldad and Medad, had remained in the camp. They were listed among the elders, but did not go out to the Tent. Yet the Spirit also rested on them, and they prophesied in the camp" (Numbers 11:24-26 NIV).

Joshua got upset about these two men prophesying, but Moses makes this statement:

"But Moses replied, "Are you jealous for my sake? I wish that all the Lord's people were prophets and that the Lord would put his Spirit on them!" (Numbers 11:29 NIV).

The prophets throughout the Tanakh announced that this statement would happen. One of the prophets was the prophet, Joel.

In addition, something very important happened. A **change in leadership** occurred. Moses was no longer a single leader. The leadership that Moses had was now delegated among the seventy elders, with Moses as the head. Numbers 11 was the proof-text used to produce the Jewish Sanhedrin.

"Israel served the Lord throughout the lifetime of Joshua and of the elders who outlived him and who had experienced everything the Lord had done for Israel" (Joshua 24:31 NIV).

This is the status at the end of Joshua. His type of leadership did not survive past the first generation. History now moves into the book of Judges.

"And also all that generation were gathered unto their fathers: and there arose another generation after them, which knew not the LORD, nor yet the works which he had

done for Israel. And the children of Israel did evil in the sight of the LORD, and served Baalim" (Judges 2:10-11 KJV).

The entire book of Judges lists this change in leadership – that of the judges. Each time Israel fell into sin, God would punish them with their enemies. They would repent, and God would send a deliverer or judge to deliver them, but the end of the book tells the results:

"In those days, there was no king in Israel: every man did that which was right in his own eyes" (Judges 21:25 KJV).

This brings the history into the book of 1 Samuel.

"Then Samuel took a vial of oil, and poured it upon his head, and kissed him, and said, Is it not because the LORD hath anointed thee to be captain over his inheritance?" (1 Samuel 10:1 KJV)

Samuel, the last judge and first prophet, is talking to Saul, who would become the King of Israel. By anointing Saul, this became another **change in leadership**. After anointing Saul and giving him several signs, Samuel tells Saul what will happen to him.

"And the Spirit of the LORD will come upon thee, and thou shalt prophesy with them, and shalt be turned into another man. And let it be, when these signs are come unto thee, that thou do as occasion serve thee; for God is with thee" (1 Samuel 10:6-7 KJV).

Did it happen?

"And when they came thither to the hill, behold, a company of prophets met him; and the Spirit of God came upon him, and he prophesied among them. And it came to pass, when all that knew him beforetime saw that, behold, he prophesied among the prophets, then the people said one to another, What is this that is come unto the son of Kish? Is Saul also among the prophets?" (1 Samuel 10-11 KJV)

Later, after this experience, King Saul receives his mission: to destroy the Ammonites.

Peter said, in Acts 2:29]-30 that David was a prophet, and scripture says he was a *"man after God's own heart"* (1 Samuel 13:14). This forces the question: why was this experience given to Saul, not David? When you read the entire tenth chapter of 1 Samuel, you find this process is connected to another change in leadership. Saul was the start of the change. David existed in the change.

Israel's kings lead the people into idolatry, and God placed them into exile, under another change in leadership: their enemies. They were under that physical leadership until May 1948.

During the four hundred years between the Tanakh and the *Brit Hadashah*, the leadership under their enemies changed in both form and function. It started with the priest and kingship of the Hosamanons, and ending with the formation of the *Sanhedrin,* with two Rabbis as its head. One was called the *"President,"* and the other was called the *"Head of the Sanhedrin"*.

The last two rabbis were Hillel and Shammai. It is also during this time, that two major parties came into being. The Sadducees, who controlled the temple and all its functions, and the Pharisees, who taught the people in the towns by means of a *"synagogue."*

We now pick up this teaching in the *Brit Hadashah*, but not in the book of Acts.

"Now when the owner of the vineyard comes, what will he do to those tenants?

They answered him, "He will viciously destroy those vicious men and rent out the vineyard to other tenants who will give him his share of the crop when it's due."

*"Yeshua said to them, 'Haven't you ever read in the Tanakh, `The very rock which the builders rejected has become the cornerstone! This has come from ADONAI, and in our eyes it is amazing? Therefore, I tell you that the Kingdom of God will **be taken away from you and given***

to the kind of people *[emphasis mine] that will produce its fruit!'"* (Matthew 21:40-43 CJB)

The word, *"nation,"* has as its Greek word, *"ethnos."* One of its meanings is a non-Jewish nation. Some Gentile churches, using these verses as proof text, teach that God had removed the covenant from the Jewish people and given it to the Gentile church.

What if they are right? It means that Yeshua, by going against the Torah, was a rebellious son, making Him a sinner, therefore not God, or it means that God has no problem breaking His covenant. Either choice should make everyone fear, not just the unbelievers.

There is another meaning to *"ethnos,"* which is *"tribe,"* or *"a group of people."* Yeshua is not applying verse 43 to the Jewish nation, but to its leadership. There was going to be another **change in leadership:**

"On one occasion, while he was eating with them, he gave them this command:" " *'Do not leave Jerusalem, but wait for the gift my Father promised, which you have heard me speak about. For John baptized with water, but in a few days you will be baptized with the <u>Ruach Hakodesh</u> [my translation].'"*

"So when they met together, they asked him, 'Lord, are you at this time going to restore the kingdom to Israel?' He said to them: 'It is not for you to know the times or dates the Father has set by his own authority. But you will receive power when the <u>Ruach Hakodesh</u> [my translation] comes on you; and you will be my witnesses in Jerusalem, and in all Judea and Samaria, and to the ends of the earth'" (Acts 1:4-8 NIV).

Acts1: 8 gives four places where they will be a witness: Jerusalem, all Judea, Samaria, and the end of the earth. It also shows grace and is not conditional. The purpose of the Power of the Holy Spirit is not just for you to demonstrate, but also for a higher calling. The Scripture says, *"You will be my witnesses."* This reality of this scripture had its start ten days later. The new **change in leadership** occurred in Acts 2:1-4:

"The festival of Shavu'ot arrived, and the believers all gathered together in one place. Suddenly there came a sound from the sky like the roar of a violent wind, and it filled the whole house where they were sitting. Then they saw what looked like tongues of fire, which separated and came to rest on each one of them. They were all filled with the Ruach HaKodesh and began to talk in different languages, as the Spirit enabled them to speak" (CJB).

The prophets spoke about this movement in the Tanakh. Instead of just an individual or a small group of people, this movement was to touch all believers. This was also the change in leadership that Yeshua talked about in Matthew 21:40-43. This change went from the temple building to the Spirit of God dwelling in man. It now begins to move out. Starting in Jerusalem, then moving to all Judea, but as of yet, this *baptism* has not reached Samaria.

In Acts 8:14-17, the *baptism* reached Samaria.

"Now when the apostles that were at Jerusalem heard that Samaria had received the word of God, they sent unto them Peter and John: who, when they were come down, prayed for them, that they might receive the <u>Ruach Hakodesh</u> [my translation]: for as yet it was fallen upon none of them: only they had been baptized into the name of the Lord <u>Yeshua</u> [my translation. Then laid they their hands on them, and they received the <u>Ruach Hakodesh</u> [my translation]" (ASV).

The Samarians were "half-breed" Jews. They were also considered idolaters. The "pure" Jews rejected them. Peter and John were considered part of the inner circle of Yeshua, with Peter as Yeshua's chief student. If the Samarians had received the *Roach Hakodesh* by the preaching of Phillip, a Greek Hellenistic Jew, the Jews in Jerusalem would have rejected it.

In the rabbinical function, the *"laying on of hands"* are used in two ways: healing, and origination into a ministry. When Peter and John, the main leaders of this Messianic movement, laid hands on the Samarians, the people received the *Ruach Hakodesh.*

The Jews in Jerusalem, knowing that Yeshua said it would happen in Acts 1:8, would not question the vitality of this experience. If a Samarian congregation and a Jewish congregation had been raised independent of each other, without the removal of the ancient and bitter barriers of prejudice between the two, the Messianic movement would have been in chaos at the very beginning of its mission.

In Acts 10:44-46, this movement goes out to the Gentile, "in the land."

"While Peter yet spake these words, the <u>Ruach Hakodesh</u> [my translation] fell on all them that heard the word."

"And they of the circumcision that believed were amazed, as many as came with Peter, because that on the Gentiles also was poured out the gift of the <u>Ruach Hakodesh</u> [my translation]."

"For they heard them speak with tongues, and magnify God" (ASV).

What happened here? Again, God chose Peter. The context shows that it took a special act of God to get Peter to enter a Gentile home. It also took a special act of God for Peter to accept it. When Peter is defending himself for baptizing the Gentiles, he says this:

"And as I began to speak, the <u>Ruach Hakodesh</u> [my translation] fell on them, even as on us at the beginning. And I remembered the word of the Lord, how he said, John indeed baptized with water; but ye shall be baptized in the <u>Ruach Hakodesh</u> [my translation]. If then God gave unto them the like gift as [he did] also unto us, when we believed on <u>Yeshua, the Messiah</u> [my translation], who was I, that I could withstand God? And when they heard these things,

they held their peace, and glorified God, saying, Then to the Gentiles also hath God granted repentance unto life" (Acts 11:15-18 ASV).

Peter recognized that God gave the same gift to the Gentiles that he experienced in Acts 2, also fulfilling Acts 1:8.

In Acts 19:1-7 this movement expands to believers "out of the land."

"And it came to pass, that, while Apollos was at Corinth, Paul having passed through the upper country came to Ephesus, and found certain disciples: and he said unto them, Did ye receive the <u>*Ruach Hakodesh*</u> *[my translation] when ye believed? And they [said] unto him, Nay, we did not so much as hear whether the* <u>*Ruach Hakodesh*</u> *[my translation] was [given]. And he said, Into what then were ye baptized? And they said, Into John's baptism."*

"And Paul said, John baptized with the baptism of repentance, saying unto the people that they should believe on him that should come after him, that is, on Jesus. And when they heard this they were baptized into the name of <u>*Yeshua, the Messiah*</u> *[my translation]. And when Paul had laid his hands upon them the* <u>*Ruach Hakodesh*</u> *[my translation] came on them; and they spake with tongues, and prophesied. And they were in all about twelve men"* (ASV).

What are the two differences between this last record of the receiving of the *Ruach Hakodesh*, and the first three times? It was not Peter, but Paul, the apostle to the Gentiles, who laid hands on them, and it was to the believers out of the land that received the *Ruach Hakodesh*.

Why is this important? The teaching that existed until this time within the orthodox Jewish circles was that God blesses the Jewish believers **in** the land, but will not bless the Jews outside the land. They are in rejection of the Torah and cursed. The Talmud teaches that only those who died in the land of Israel will rise on the last day. This Scripture shows this teaching to be in error.

Acts 10 was to **Gentiles in** the land. This scripture was to **believers outside** the land, proving God does apply His blessings to believers who are outside the land. This also become a fulfillment of Acts 1:8

Again, how do you receive the *Ruach Hakodesh?* Acts 2:38-39 gives the three steps:

"And Peter [said] unto them, Repent ye, and be baptized every one of you in the name of <u>Yeshua the Messiah</u> [my translation] unto the remission of your sins; and ye shall receive the gift of the <u>Ruach Hakodesh</u> [my translation]. For to you is the promise, and to your children, and to all that are afar off, [even] as many as the Lord our God shall call unto him" (ASV).

First, repent: go one hundred and eighty degrees from where you are going. Second, accept Yeshua as your Messiah. Third, be baptized. This promise is not for only one generation, but carries forward to the future. It is not only for those in the land of Israel, but around the world. If you fulfilled these three requirements, you have the *Ruach Hakodesh* within you.

Scripture calls your receiving the *Ruach Hakodesh* as the "down payment" of your God given inheritance. You can think of it as a credit card. When you "raise your credit score" by these three steps, you receive the *Ruach Hakodesh* as the "credit card" of your inheritance. You have the card, but it must be activated. This is done when you move out in faith, as recorded in Galatians 3:2, to help build God's kingdom. This act, done for this purpose, will change your life, both individually and corporately.

Appendix 2 – The Power Of Psalm 91

For 21 years, from July 31, 1930 to December 26, 1954, people listened to a radio program, which was part of the *"Detective Story Hour,"* called *"The Shadow."*

If you are old enough to remember, you were glued to your chair, waiting to hear those chilling words opening the program: *"Who knows what evil lurks in the hearts of men? The Shadow knows!"* There is another shadow in scripture that this line can be applied.

"He who dwells in the shelter of the Most High will rest in the shadow of the Almighty. I will say of the Lord, 'He is my refuge and my fortress, my God, in whom I trust'" (Psalm 91:1-2 NIV).

"Every good and perfect gift is from above, coming down from the Father of the heavenly lights, who does not change like shifting shadows" (James 1:17 NIV).

With these verses in mind, consider this question: what or where is God's shadow? Psalm 91 talks about *"God's shadow,"* but James 1:17 says God has no shadow. A number of scholars believe God's shadow is the power, or the anointing, of God.

Psalm 91 tells about the protection given to believers who *"dwell in the secret place"* (Psalm 91:1 NIV). The "secret place" is scripture study and prayer. Scripture study and prayer equals fellowship with God because of what Yeshua has done. If you outline the ninety-first Psalm, it would be in three sections: the conditions, who is the person doing the protection, and the extent of that protection.

Who is the protector? His Name represents all of God's Glory. There are *four* names of God given in the first two verses. They are:

1) *"The Most High"* which, in Hebrew, is *"Elyone,"* meaning *"lofty and supreme."*

2) *"Almighty"* in Hebrew is *"Shaddai,"* meaning *"the Strong and Mighty One."*

3) *"Lord,"* which, in Hebrew, is not pronounced by the Jewish people; but is called *"HaShem"* or *"The Name."* This is the "I AM" given to Moses at the burning bush. It means "I will be with you wherever you go";

4) *"God"*, which in Hebrew is *"Elohim,"* the Creator who made the world from nothing, and the Supreme God of Israel.

How would you like to have Him on your side as your protector? What is the extent of that protection? Read Psalm 91 and allow the anointing of God to give understanding. Verse 3 to verse 16 gives you the power of God's deliverance and protection. It informs you, in verse 5, that you are protected from some attacks you are not aware exists.

In Verse 7, it teaches that the ones who fall on your right and left sides are not your enemies, because you normally face, or run from enemies, but other believers who did not fulfill the conditions of the first two verses. In verse 13, it talks about protection from the enemies of your soul.

The most powerful verses in this Psalm are verses 14-16. The personal noun of these verses changes from "He" to "I". God Himself is speaking through the mouth of the psalmist, showing how the extent of God's protection is awesome!

Consider this:

You are protected by God from attacks on your front by verses 3,4,5 & 9; and you are protected from your back by verses 3,5 & 9;

You are protected by God from attacks on your right side by verses 3, 7 & 9; and you are protected on your left side by verses 3, 7 & 9;

You are protected by God from your top by verses 3,4,5 & 9; and you are protected from your bottom by verses 3,4,9 & 13;

You are protected by God during the day by verses 3,5,6 & 9; and you are protected during the night by verses 3,5,6 & 9;

You are protected by God inside your home by verses 3,9 & 10; and you are protected outside your home by verses 3,10 & 14;

Best of all, you are protected in this life by verses 8,11,15 & 16; and you are protected in the life to come by verse 16. Indeed, God's protection is awesome!

Appendix 3 – Paul's Concept Of The "Law"

What was Paul's concept of the law (Torah)? Was Paul a hypocrite? Or was he a good teacher of the Word of God? There are only two answers to that last question: yes or no. If the answer is yes, you should follow what he says. If the answer is no, it makes him a false teacher, and you should reject what he says.

The answer to this question will determine your doctrine, just like it did Marcion, who was declared a heretic, and was excommunicated in 144 C.E. His interpretation of Isaiah 45:7 was fundamental to his doctrine. It reads:

"I form the light, and create darkness: I make peace, and create evil: I the LORD do all these things" (KJV).

By this one verse, he reasoned that an evil tree is not able to produce good fruit. So he concluded that there are two gods: the Creator God of the "Old Testament," who was fickle and cruel, and the Supreme God of the "New Testament" who was a God of love as revealed in Yeshua. He rejected the entire Tanakh, and would only accept the Gospel of Luke. Yet, he still edited out all references to the Tanakh. In his gospel, there was no prophecies or Jewish historical events.

For Marcion, the only true apostle was Paul. He believed the other apostles had corrupted Yeshua's teachings by adding legalism. He took ten of Paul's epistles, excluding 1 & 2 Timothy and Titus, and removed any verse showing "Jewish corruptions." This is how he handled Paul's concept of the "law."

Some people, like Marcion, ignore or forget some scriptures while creating doctrines from others. This creates an unbalanced view of the Word of God. How can the "Old Testament" be "old" when seventy-eight percent of it is unfulfilled? How can the "New Testament" be "new" when ninety-six percent of its quotations come from the Tanakh?

Let me explain what I call: "the *trap*." Please open your Bible, and read the verses quoted. I used the NASB version. Please use this version, King James or the NIV. Why? It will be the version most church people will use.

	CON		PRO
Eph. 2:15	The law (*Torah*) is Abolished	Romans 3:31	The law (*Torah*) has been established
Romans 7:6	You have been "discharged from the law" (*Torah*)	Romans 7:12	The law (*Torah*) is "holy, just and good" (Note: This statement is in the same chapter)
Romans 10:4	The Messiah is "the *end* of the law (*Torah*)"	Romans 8:3-4	The just requirements of the law (*Torah*) are "fulfilled in us"

Romans 3:28	The "law (*Torah*) is unnecessary"	1 Cor. 7:19	The "law (*Torah*) is necessary" Note: This can also be found in Ephesians 6:2-3 and 1 Timothy 1:8-10
2 Cor. 3:7	The law (*Torah*) is the "dispensation of death"	Romans 3:2	The law (*Torah*) is part of "the oracles of God" entrusted to the Jews.

Before we continue, I must again state that it is not my goal or intention to "church-bash" a doctrine or belief. It is my intention to show the context of the scriptures.

All of these scriptures come from the writings of one man, Paul, and were written to one group of people: Gentiles. These verses cannot be used against the Jewish people. You will be *"reading someone else's mail."* Based on this new information, I am again going to ask the same question: was Paul a good teacher of the Word of God, or was he a hypocrite?

If Paul was a good teacher, how do you explain the differences in his understanding of the law (*Torah*)? If your answer is *"He was all things to all people so that he might win some,"* paraphrasing 1 Corinthians 9:22, you have declared

Paul a hypocrite. If Paul was a hypocrite, than he was also a false teacher. If he was a false teacher, than why should you follow what he says?

If you believe Paul was a good teacher, you must be able to explain the differences. You must be able to answer this very important question. Why? If you approach a Jewish person about his Messiah, showing him, without his knowledge, the **pro** side of scriptures written for Gentiles, along with the rest of scriptures in the Tanakh about the Messiah, he will strongly consider your statements.

Here is the problem. What happens when the Jewish person reads, or is shown the **con** side of the scriptures by his rabbi, who does not believe that Yeshua is the Messiah? He will, without an answer of the differences, classify Paul as a false teacher, and will reject the scriptures, and his Messiah.

If a church-going believer shows the Jewish person the **con** side in an attempt to change him into a Gentile believer, he will, again, classify Paul as a false teacher.

If he is shown both sides of the coin at the same time, and given a solid answer as to the differences, he is more available to accept Yeshua as the Jewish Messiah.

Again, based on this new information, was Paul a good teacher of the Word of God, or was he a hypocrite? The answer is that Paul was a good teacher, but this forces the question: how do you handle the contradiction? Allow me to explain.

When the Scriptures are read in context, you will find Paul dealing with two types of believers: first, look at the **con** side. It involves the Gentile believers, and their salvation. The words "salvation" or "justification" means "*right standing before God.*" Paul was teaching against the instructions of "Yeshua **plus** _____ (you fill in the blank)" for salvation.

As written in another chapter, in all of Paul's writings, the word "*justification*" is used over eighty times when applied to the Gentile. The word "*repentance*" was never used. This word was only applied to the Jews. Why? The word, "*repentance*" means, "*returning to where you came from,*" which implies *T'shuvah*, but if it were applied to the Gentile, it would require them to return to idol worship.

The second type of believer involves the **pro** side, dealing with the Gentile believers and their conduct after salvation. To cover the pro side, another word is used: "*sanctification,*" which means, "*right living before God.*" It is at this position that repentance is also applied to the Gentile.

When Yeshua said to His apostles to "*make disciples of all nations,*" He was talking about Gentiles. A disciple is one who follows the teachings and the life of his master, in our case, Yeshua. Yeshua, a Jew, followed the law (*Torah, meaning God's instructions and teachings.*) It was this process Paul was teaching as it applied to the Gentiles.

Appendix 4 – The Word "New"

The word "new" has been used by a large number of believers to show that the elect is the new Israel. This teaching became doctrine through Augustine around the fifth century. Is this doctrine true?

Consider these Scriptures:

*"Behold, the days come, saith the LORD, that I will make a **new** [chadash] [emphasis mine] covenant with the house of Israel, and with the house of Judah"* (Jeremiah 31:31 KJV).

*"A new heart also will I give you, and a **new** [chadah] [emphasis mine] spirit will I put within you: and I will take away the stony heart out of your flesh, and I will give you a heart of flesh.*

And I will put my spirit within you, and cause you to walk in my statutes, and ye shall keep my judgments, and do them" (Ezekiel 36:26-27 KJV).

Check out Hebrews:

*"For finding fault with them, he saith, Behold, the days come, saith the Lord, when I will make a **new** [emphasis mine] covenant with the house of Israel and with the house of Judah"* (Hebrews 8:8 KJV).

Hebrews is quoting Jeremiah 31:31. Why is this important? These verses are used by a number of churches as proof texts for the super covenant theology. This doctrine states that God made a covenant with the faithful elect. The argument goes like this:

- The new covenant was made with the elect in Israel
- The elect is the church
- If that is so, it means the church is the elect
- This means the church is Israel

So the conclusion is the new covenant was made with the church. To understand how this doctrine became the *"New Israel,"* you must go to its history.

Justin Martyr was the first person that believed that the church was the true Israel; but not in the replacement sense as it is applied today.

This can be seen in his *"Dialogue with Trypho the Jew,"* around 160 C.E. He is the first to apply the title "Spiritual Jew" to the elect.[59]

The man responsible for the replacement sense of this doctrine was a man named Origen. He was considered one of the church's first theologians.

Origen, who lived between 185 – 254 C.E., was considered the father of the allegorical system of interpretation of scriptures. In doing so, he rejected the literal context of the scriptures and replaced it with his allegories, which he made up. The allegories could not be debated or challenged on scriptures because the text used was said to be no longer what it meant. It was through his teachings that the Jews were disinherited from the blessings of the covenant and the blessings were given to the church.

Origen, because of his teachings and doctrines, was declared by two church councils as a heretic and was excommunicated in 331 and 332 C.E. The church fathers rejected his teachings and doctrines but they kept his allegorical system.

Origen had a pupil named Pamphilus. He had a pupil and friend named Eusebius, who spent a great deal of his life defending the views of Origen. During his lifetime, Eusebius wrote a six-volume defense of Origin's teachings. He wanted to convince the church that Origen was correct. He also applied this purpose when he defended Origen in his book, *Ecclesiastical History*, the history of the church covering from the end of the book of Acts to the Council of Nicea.

Eusebius had a friend from childhood, who saw how devoted he was to the teachings of Origen: Constantine. Origen's heresy became doctrine in the Council of Nicea through Eusebius, Constantine, and those who followed them.

Here is the problem. Making a covenant with only the elect is to take the covenant from the Jews and give it to the church. God does not speak of making a covenant **only** with the faithful elect, but with all of Israel and Judah. This "super covenant" doctrine stands or falls on the interpretating the word "new."

Consider this question: Does the word "new" mean "new in time" or "new in character or quality?" This is not a stupid question. The entire "super covenant" doctrine is based on the answer. *"New in time"* makes the covenant a brand new covenant, while *"new in character or quality"* makes the covenant a renewed covenant. It means that the original covenant still exists, but some part changed in its character or quality. For the "super covenant" to stand, the word "new" must mean "new in time." Does it?

In Jeremiah 31:31, the Hebrew word for "new" is *"chadash"*. Its primary sense is that of cutting a diamond or polishing. The signification of newness appears to proceed from a sharp, polished sword. It means to renew, restore, restart, or repair. This meaning of renew or restore can be seen in 1 Samuel 11:14; Job 10:17; and Psalm 51:12. In Isaiah 61:4, the word, *"chadash"* is applied to repair or restore buildings or towns. In Psalm 103:5, it is applied to renew yourself.

Ezekiel 36:26-27 also uses the word *"chadash"* for the word "new." It states that the heart will be made "new" by the process of changing from a heart of stone to a heart of flesh. This is not a brand new heart; it is changed from the character or quality of "stone" to the character or quality of "flesh."

Now let's look at the *Brit Hadashah*. In Luke 22:20, it reads:

"Likewise also the cup after supper, saying, This cup is the new testament in my blood, which is shed for you" (KJV).

This same verse is recorded in Matthew 26:28 and Mark 14:24. In these two Scriptures, it is missing one word: "new."

There are three words for the word "new" in Greek. They are *"kianos," "neos,"* and *"prosphatos."* When you look in the *Vines Expository Dictionary of New Testament Words*, it gives the meaning of *"kianos"* as "not new in time, but new as to form or quality." The Greek word *"neos"* is translated as "new in respect to time, recent or numerically new."

The Greek word, *"prosphatos"* is translated as "freshly slain, in the sense of being new." This word is used in Hebrews 10:20.

The Greek translation for the Hebrew word *"chadash"* is "kainos," meaning, "renewed." Most of the *Brit Hadashah* Scriptures use *"kainos"* for "new." A few Scriptures use *"neos."* Here is an example of each:

*"Therefore if any man be in <u>the Messiah</u> [my translation], he is a **new** [kainos][emphasis mine] creature: old things are passed away; behold, all things are become **new** [kainos] [emphasis mine]"* (2 Corinthians 5:17 KJV).

*"And have put on the **new** [neos][emphasis mine] man, which is **renewed** [a derivative of kainos][emphasis mine] in knowledge after the image of him that created him"* (Colossians 3:10 KJV).

The superstructure cannot exceed the foundation. The body of the Messiah is '...*built on the foundation of apostles and prophets, The <u>Messiah Yeshua</u> [my translation] Himself being the chief cornerstone"* (Ephesians 2:20 KJV). Removing scripture from its context does not build the foundation.

Appendix 5 – Yeshua, The Living Torah

It has been said that if Yeshua cannot be found in every section of the Torah, He cannot be the Living Torah. If He can be found in the Torah, than he is your King and Master. When you look through the Torah, can you find Him in every portion?

We accept five Books as the Torah. In *"Bereishit"* (Genesis), this King is your covenant-maker. In *"Shemot"* (Exodus), He is your covenant-keeper. In *"Vayikra"* (Leviticus, He is your boundary-setter. In *"Bamidbar"* (Numbers), He is your protector and provider. Also, in *"Devarim"* (Deuteronomy), He is your rabbi and your king;

There are fifty-four *Parshas* in the Torah. The twelve *Parshas* of Genesis can be compared to the foundation of the twelve tribes and the twelve apostles. The eleven *Parshas* of Exodus and Deuteronomy can be compared to the eleven spices that, according to the Talmud (Tractate *Keritot*), make up the incense. This represents the prayers of the believers. The ten *Parshas* of Leviticus and Numbers can be compared to the Ten Commandments and two divisions.

Parshas Of The Torah

Let's look at each of the fifty-four *Parshas* in the Torah and see who this King is that you serve.

In Parsha 1 of Genesis, *Bereishit* (*"In the beginning"*), He is seen as your Creator (*"Memra"* meaning *"Word"*); He is also the Spirit of God that hovers above the water.

In Parsha 2, *Noach* ("Noah"), He is a picture of Noah's Ark: a place of safety. He was promised to come from the line of Shem. He is seen in the number seven, which is represented by the seven colors of the rainbow and is seen in Noah's offering.

In *Parsha* 3, *Lech Lecha* ("Get yourself out"), He is the King-Priest after the order of Melchizedek, and His name is "Peace."

In *Parsha* 4, *Vayeira* ("He appeared"), He is Isaac's sacrifice: the tenth test of Abraham. He is seen in the miracle of His birth, which is after the order of Isaac; He is seen in Abraham's ram and the angel who stopped Abraham and blessed him.

In *Parsha* 5, *Chayei Sarah* ("Sarah's life"), He is the Bridegroom, and you are a part of the bride as seen through the marriage of Isaac and Rebecca.

In *Parsha* 6, *Toldos* ("History"), He is sovereign in choosing you.

In *Parsha* 7, *Vayeitzei* ("He went out"), He is seen as Jacob's ladder. He is also seen as the living water at Jacob's well.

In *Parsha* 8, *Vayishlach* ("He sent"), He is seen as the angel who wrestled with Jacob and blessed him. Again, He is seen in the place called *"Peniel,"* which means *"the face of God."*

In *Parsha* 9, *Vayeishev* ("He continued living"), He is a type of Joseph: favored by his father, rejected by his brothers, sold for the price of a slave. He is seen in Judah's staff. Because of her righteousness, Tamar, a woman, is added to His genealogy line.

In *Parsha* 10, *Mikeitz* ("At the end"), He is seen through the names of Manasseh and Ephraim. He is the Savior of his family. Like Judah, He is your spokesman and your guarantor.

In *Parsha* 11, *Vayigash* ("He approached"), He has the descriptive names of "Memra," "Savior," "Immanuel," and the "Son of Man."

In *Parsha* 12, *Vayechi* ("He lived"), He is *"Shiloh"* (your Peacemaker), and He is the Lion of Judah.

Who is this King that you serve?

In *Parsha* 1 of Exodus, *Shemot* ("Names"), He is the One in the burning bush: the "I AM". He is the angel who met Moses on the way back to Egypt.

In *Parsha* 2, *Va'eira* ("I appeared"), you am set apart by Him; He is your Savior. He is seen in the third cup of redemption at Passover, and seen in Moses' rod. He is the One who fights for you.

In *Parsha* 3, *Bo* ("Go"), He is seen as your Passover Lamb, your blood covering, your "*Afikomen*", your bitter herbs, and your circumcision.

In *Parsha* 4, *Beshalach* ("After he had let go"), He is seen as the Mikvah, as the Rock that produces living water, as the Manna: the food of God, and as Moses' rod.

In *Parsha* 5, *Yisro* ("Jethro"), He is the Living Torah itself, and seen as the Bridegroom.

In *Parsha* 6, *Mishpatim* ("Rulings"), He is the Righteous One, the dispenser and demonstrator of Torah, and the angel that was to lead Israel into the Promised Land.

In *Parsha* 7, *Terumah* ("Contribution"), He is seen in the floor plan of the Mishkan itself: the Ark of the Covenant, the Holy Place, the outside court, the acacia wood, the curtain in the Holy Place, the table of shewbread, the menorah, the altar of incense, the altar of sacrifice, and the silver foundation.

In *Parsha* 8, *Tetzaveh* ("You are to order"), He is seen in the copper laver. He is your God-appointed High Priest, the breastplate of Aaron, and your headpiece that says "Holiness Unto the Lord."

In *Parsha* 9, *Ki Sisa* ("When you take"), He is your reconciliation. He is seen in the thirteen attributes of God.

In *Parsha* 10, *Vayakhel* ("He assembled") He is seen in the number seven, and He is the visible presence of God called the "*Shchinah*."

In *Parsha* 11, *Pekudei* ("Accounts"), as your bridegroom, He brings you to His home.

Who is this King that you serve?

In *Parsha* 1 of Leviticus, *Vayikra* ("He called"), He is seen as your burnt offering, your meal offering, your peace offering, your sin offering, and your guilt offering.

In *Parsha* 2, *Tzav* ("Give an order"), He is your Anointing. He is seen in the oil and the blood of the sacrifice.

In *Parsha* 3, *Shemini* ("Eighth"), He is your Holiness, and He is your number eight, which speaks of new beginnings.

In *Parsha* 4, *Tazria* ("She conceives"), He is the One who makes you clean, who gives you life.

In *Parsha* 5, *Metzora* ("Person afflicted with tzara'at"), He is seen as your healer.

In *Parsha* 6, *Acharei Mot* ("After the death"), He is your blood atonement, your life carrier, and your Yom Kippur. He is seen in the red ribbon turning white.

In *Parsha* 7, *Kedoshim* ("Holy People"), He is your Holiness; He guides your walk.

In *Parsha* 8, *Emor* ("Speak"), He is seen in the *Passover* feast, in the Sabbath, in the *Unleavened Bread*, in the *First Fruits*, in *Shavuot*, in *Sukkot*, and in *Rosh Hashanah*.

In *Parsha* 9, *Behar* ("On Mount"), He is your Jubilee, your freedom, your provider, and your "*Go-El*" (Kinsman Redeemer).

In *Parsha* 10, *Bechukosai* ("By My regulations"), He is seen as your judge, your Savior, your covenant-maker, and your mikvah. He is seen as God's sword. He is seen in the loaf of living bread and the rod that disciplines you.

Who is this King that you serve?

In *Parsha* 1 of Numbers, *Bamidbar* ("In the desert"), He is seen in the orders of the Levites. He is the head of God's army and God's firstborn.

In *Parsha* 2, *Nasso* ("Take"), He is your high priest who blesses, and is your guilt offering.

In *Parsha* 3, *Beha'aloscha* ("When you set up"), He is the Prophet like Moses, and the One who sanctifies you.

In *Parsha* 4, *Shelach* ("Send on your behalf"), He gives you your new name, and He is your *Tzitzis*.

In *Parsha* 5, *Korach* ("Korah"), He is seen as Aaron's rod, your intercessor, and He stands between life and death for you.

In *Parsha* 6, *Chukas* ("Regulation"), He is seen as your red heifer, as your brass serpent, and is seen again as the Rock that gives your children living water.

In *Parsha* 7, *Balak* ("Balak"), He is seen as the Angel that delivers the Word, and as the Star of Jacob.

In *Parsha* 8, *Pinchas* ("Phinehas"), He is the One who gives you the covenant of peace.

In *Parsha* 9, *Mattos* ("Tribes"), He lays out the boundaries of your life.

In *Parsha* 10, *Masei* ("Stages"), He is your place of refuse and safety. He is your Protection when you unintentionally sin.

Who is this King that you serve?

In *Parsha* 1 of Deuteronomy, *Devarim* ("Words"), He is your Torah-teacher.

In *Parsha* 2, *Va'eschanan* ("I pleaded"), He is seen in the Shama, seen in the Ten Commandments, and seen as your place of refuge and safety. He gives you the rewards of the Covenant.

In *Parsha* 3, *Eikev* ("Because"), He is the One who gives you power for success. He is seen in the four Names of God (Deuteronomy 7:21). He is your "*Soul Food.*"

In *Parsha* 4, *Re'eh* ("See"), He is your Torah, where nothing is added or subtracted. He is where God placed His Name. He teaches you accountability; He is your "Kosher Rabbi."

In *Parsha* 5, *Shoftim* ("Judges"), He is your King, and your war-priest; He is the perfect sacrifice, and your safe haven. He is seen again as your Judge.

In *Parsha* 6, *Ki Seitzei* ("When you go out"), He gives you the inheritance of the first-born. He is seen again as your Torah teacher.

In *Parsha* 7, *Ki Savo* ("When you come"), He is the One who gives you blessings. He is the first-fruit of God. He gives you His Name. He took the curses and paid the price for you.

In *Parsha* 8, *Nitzavim* ("Standing"), He is the One who ratifies the new covenant.

In *Parsha* 9, *Vayeilech* ("He went"), He is your encourager.

In *Parsha* 10, *Haazinu* ("Hear"), He is your witness and your "*Sabbath of Return.*"

In *Parsha* 11, *Vezos Haberachah* ("This is the blessing"), He is your Alpha and Omega, the Beginning and the End. He is seen as your *Simchat Torah*.

Who is this King that you serve?

He Is *Yeshua, HaMashiach:* the Son Of The Living God!

Behold your King is coming to you! How are you going to receive Him?

XI. ABOUT THE AUTHOR

R onald Warren, respected Messianic Jewish lecturer and writer, brings his lifelong passion for scriptural study and biblical history to students seeking deeper knowledge of the Hebraic path of faith.

Prior to co-founding a Messianic congregation in 2002, Ronald taught study classes for another Messianic congregation in Orlando, and devoted his studies to become a Messianic Rabbi. He established *Simchat Torah*, a Messianic bible study group in Kissimmee, Florida. This later led him to become one of the principle founders and the spiritual leader of a Messianic congregation in Casselberry, Florida. Within two years, this congregation experienced substantial growth.

In 2004, God began opening another door while closing the door behind him. After much prayer and seeking the will of the Lord, Ronald understood that his calling was not to become a Pastoral Rabbi of a Messianic congregation but a Messianic bible teacher, lecturer, and author, and be accessible to all who would seek the true gospel of Messiah.

At the same time, God was preparing a replacement for this congregation. The President of the *Messianic Jewish Alliance of America* (MJAA), Rabbi Charles Kluge, Leader of *Melech Yisrael* in West Palm Beach, Florida, was being led by God to relocate to central Florida. After many meetings and much prayer, the board, led by Ron, turned the leadership over to Rabbi Charles Kluge, and a new congregation was established called *Gesher Shalom* (Bridge of Peace).

Ronald now devotes more time to completing his Messianic teaching studies, as well as lecturing and writing about the application of Scripture from a strict Hebraic understanding. Today he is a regular speaker at churches throughout the central Florida area.

Ronald's regular email-based newsletter, "The Scribe's Journal," is currently read and enjoyed by subscribers throughout North America, Europe, and Asia. In addition, he maintains and moderates *"Simchat Torah Institute,"* an internet-based website and discussion forum for Messianic students.

Ronald Warren and his wife, JoAnn, are today active members of *Gesher Shalom*, a large Messianic Jewish community based in central Florida. They currently reside, with their two sons, in Orlando, Florida.

For more information about Mr. Warren and his work (including newsletter and forum information), please visit Simchat-Torah-Institute on the Web at http://www. simchat-torah-institute.com. Mr. Warren himself can be reached via email at RonWarren@torahlifepublishing.com or Torahlife@ usa.net

XII   End Notes

I.   <u>What this Book can do for You</u>

Faith is Embedded in Trust
1. This book was published in 1865 to entertain Alice Liddell, daughter of the Dean of Christ Church. In the notes of Martin Gardner placed in the book, he states that this line may have come from the Talmud. (Lewis Carroll, *"The Annotated Alice: Alice's Adventures in Wonderland,"* A work by Martin Gardner, incorporating the text of Lewis Carroll, W.W. Norton & Company, Inc., 500 Fifth Avenue, New York, NY 10110; copyright 1960; page 66)

II.   <u>Yeshua – Jacob's Ladder</u>

Yeshua as the Ladder
2. First Fruits of Zion Torah Club, Volume two, *"Yeshua in the Torah,"* Parsha *"Vayeitzei,"* Page 3, First Fruits of Zion, 6657 W. Ottawa Place, Unit A-4, Littleton, CO 80123
3. Ibid., 3
4. Ibid., 3

Yahweh (YHWH) – The Problem

5. This can be found on the Internet searching on goggle for the keyword, "Yahweh." It is located at "http:// en.wikipedia.org/wiki/tetragrammaton"

What is Worship?

6. The New Webster Dictionary of the English Language: International Edition, *"Respect to Zynurgy,"* Volume two; Page 965, Grolier Incorporated, New York, Copyright 1970

III.   The Noachide Commandments

The Time Frame Problem

7. The Mishnah was done under Rabbi Judah HaNasi, in consultation with members of the Academy. Rabbis Hiyya and Oshaiah edited the Tosefta on their own; this made the Tosefta less authoritative than the Mishnah and became a 'supplement' to it.

(Messiah Magazine, Issue 91, Bamidbar 5766 (2006); First Fruits of Zion; PO Box 620099, Littleton, CO 80162; pages 10-11; the article, "The Noachide Laws" by Tim Hegg)

8. Ibid., 10-11

9. Rabbi Moshe ben Maimon (Rambam) was born in 1135 C.E. He was also known as Miamonides. He died at the age of 70. His tombstone reads, *"From Moshe to Moshe, there is none like Moshe."*

The endnotes of the Messiah Magazine listed the source as Hilchot Melachim 8:11 (R. Eliyahu Trouger, trans., *Mishneh Torah: Sefer Shoftim,* [Moanaim 2001], 582).

(Messiah Magazine, Issue 91, Bamidbar 5766 (2006); First Fruits of Zion; PO Box 620099, Littleton, CO 80162; pages 12-13; the article, *"The Noachide Laws"* by Tim Hegg)

IV   Four Types of Gentiles

The Pagan

10. This sermon was taken from an eBook put out the Jonathan Edwards Center at Yale University. This sermon was so powerful that thousands of sinners gave their hearts to Yeshua, and it was the start of the revival known as *"The Great Awaking"* in England.

If you want a copy for your records, you can get it at "http://edwards.yale.edu/major-works/sinners-in-the-hands-of-an-angry-god" or go direct to "http://edwards.yale.edu/images/pdf/sinners.pdf"

The Righteous Gentile

11. My understanding of the Greek word *"stavros"*, which is usually translated as "cross" is taken from David Stern's Commentary of the Jewish New Testament. Mr. Stern's definition of the *"Execution-stake"* literally changed and deepened my understanding of the cross.

David H. Stern, "Jewish New Testament Commentary," Jewish New Testament Publications; PO Box 1313, Clarksville, Maryland 21029, Copyright 1992, Page 40-41

Yeshua, "HaTorah"

12. First Fruits of Zion Torah Club, Volume two, *"Yeshua in the Torah,"* Parsha *"Yitro,"* Page 7, First Fruits of Zion, 6657 W. Ottawa Place, Unit A-4, Littleton, CO 80123

13. Michael L Brown, "Answering Jewish Objections to Jesus", Volume Four, Baker Books, Grand Rapids, Michigan, Copyright 2007. pages 65 – 66.In his footnotes at the end of the book, foot note #149, it lists as follows: "According to Graham Pockett's website, "http://www.anointedlinks.com/one_solitary_life.html", This essay was adapted from a sermon by Dr. James Allan Francis's sermon in the "The Real Jesus and other Sermons" (Philadelphia: Judson Press,

1926,) pp 123-124, titled "Arise, Sir Knight!" For the original text, see *"One Solitary Life,"* at "http://www.anointedlinks. com/one_solitary_life_original.html"

V. Is Yeshua the Written Word?

VI. The Leap of Faith

Three Elements of Saving Faith

14. Billy Apostolon, (*"Soul Winning Sermons,"* chapter 4, *"You Had Better Beware"* by Carl Johnson, Baker Book House, Grand Rapids, Michigan; copyright 1965; page 43-44)

15. Ibid., 52

The Four Battlefields of Faith

16. The first person to make this quote was Benjamin Franklin and can be found at "http://www.thinkexist.com." This quote was made famous by Albert Einstein and can be found on the Internet at "http://www.brainquote.com/quotes/ quotes/a/alberteins133991.html"

VII. Faith's Ladder of Trust

The Seven Applications

17. The Greek word for 'faith' is "Pistis," and can be found on page 411 of the "Vines Expository Dictionary of New Testament Words. (W.E. Vine, MA, MacDonald Publishing Company, McLean, Virginia, 22101

The Altar of Sacrifice

18. M.R. DeHaan M.D., "The Tabernacle," Zondervan Publishing House, Grand Rapids, Michigan, Copyright 1955, page 69

19. Ibid., 69

20. Ibid., 69
21. Ibid., 80
22. Ibid., 72
23. Ibid., 74

The Laver
24. Ibid., 84
25. Ibid., 86
26. Ibid., 87
27. Ibid., 88

The Table of Shewbread
28. Ibid., 92
29. Ibid., 93
30. Ibid., 93
31. Ibid., 95
32. Ibid., 95

The Menorah
33. Ibid., 97
34. Ibid., 97
35. Ibid., 98
36. Ibid., 99

The Altar of Incense
37. Ibid., 104
38. Ibid., 108
39. Ibid., 109
40. Ibid., 110

The Ark of the Covenant
41. Ibid., 119
42. Ibid., 121
43. Ibid., 121
44. Ibid., 121

45. Ibid., 122
46. Ibid., 122

The Mercy Seat
   47. Ibid., 90
   48. Ibid., 127
   49. Ibid., 127
   50. Ibid., 128
   51. Ibid., 128
   52. Ibid., 128
   53. Ibid., 131

VIII.   <u>The Ladder of Trust and your Choice</u>

She Believed
   54. Henry E Turlington, The Broadman Bible Commentary, (Nashville: Broadman Press, 1946), Vol. 8, p. 310

David and the Ladder of Trust
   55. This quote can be found on the Internet at "http://www.brainyquote.com/quotes/quotes/authors/a/abraham_lincoln.html"

If You Are Jewish
   56. Messianic High Holiday Prayer Book, compiled by Jeremiah Greenberg, Director – Messianic Liturgical Resources, PO Box 342083, Tampa, FL. 33694; Second Printing; Summer 2003; page 76
   57. Messianic Shabbat Siddur, compiled by Jeremiah Greenberg, Director – Messianic Liturgical Resources, PO Box 342083, Tampa, FL. 33694; 12th Printing; Fall 2004; page 74

58. Kevin Howard and Marvin Rosenthal; "The Feasts of the Lord"; Published by Zion's Hope, Inc., PO Box 690909, Orlando, FL. 32869; Copyright 1997; page 127

Appendix 4 – the word, "NEW"

59. Daniel Gruber, *"The Church and the Jews: The Biblical Relationship;"* copyright 1991; page 13

XIII.   SUBJECT INDEX

—~∾~—

A.

J.

Jacob, 46-47, 54-55, 58-59, 77, 185, 200, 236, 239
    Jacob (James), Jacob's (James), 78, 80-82, 85-86
    Jacob's Ladder, 43, 45, 58, 236, 245
Jehovah (also see God), 49-51, 100
Jerusalem Council, 76, 85
Jewish, 37, 39, 47-49, 59, 63-64, 59, 63-64, 67, 71-76, 78, 80, 83, 92, 99, 102, 107-109, 117, 150, 159, 185-186, 188-189, 191-192, 198, 209, 215, 218, 220-221, 224, 226, 228-229, 241-242, 247, 250
Justification, 141-142, 154, 191, 229
Judaism, 63, 97-98, 102, 113, 189-190

K.

Keritot, 159, 235
KJV (King James Bible), 33, 39, 41, 45-46, 48-55, 58-68, 73-75, 77, 79-84, 92, 98-99, 101-102, 107, 111-113, 115, 117-118, 120, 127, 129, 132, 135-138, 148-149, 151, 153, 156-157, 159, 161, 164-165, 172-175, 178-179, 182, 185, 187-188, 190-191, 193, 204, 206, 208, 214, 216, 226, 231, 234
Kosher, 240
    Kosher, Biblical, 82

L.

Ladder, 34-35, 38, 43, 45-47, 54, 58-68, 107, 111, 119, 156, 161, 168, 177, 179, 181, 236, 245
Ladder of Trust, 34, 38, 64, 92, 147-148, 150, 152-153, 156, 158-159, 161, 163, 167, 169, 171-172, 174-180, 248, 250
Laver (also see Tabernacle), 150-152, 180-183, 237, 249

S.

T.

$7000.00 Over & Over Again..

Ready for a Positive Change?

•Can you See Yourself Making Substantially Greater Income?

• Do You Value Education and Mentoring from the Richest Christian Entrepreneurial & Wealth Mentoring Environment Available?

• Are You a Self-Starter and Serious about Creating a Better Future for You and Your Family?

For Additional Information and to Download Your FREE Powerful Book, *"Slay Your Giant,"* Go To: www.acMindsetMentor.com

(Use Code *"LOT07"* for Your FREE Book, "Slay Your Giant")

No One Will Call Unless You Ask To Be Called

"And be not fashioned according to this world: but be ye transformed by the renewing of your mind, and ye may prove what is the good and acceptable and perfect will of G-d." (Romans 12:2)

Quick Order Form

Email Orders: Ron@torahlifepublishing.com
Website Orders: www.torahlifepublishing.com Have your credit card ready
Telephone Orders: Call (407) 443-5068. Have your credit card ready
Postal Orders: Torahlife Publishing, Ron Warren, 931 North State Road 434, Suite 1201-347, Altamonte Springs, Fl 32714 USA, Telephone: (407) 443-5068

Please send me the book: *The Ladder of Trust.*
Name: _____
Address: _____
City: _____
State: _____ Zip Code: _____
Telephone: _____
Email Address: _____

Total Quantity of Books:_____ Total Cost: _____
Sales Tax: Please add 6% for products shipped to Florida addresses _____

Shipping and Handling (**See Note) _____

Total Cost _____

NOTE: [Shipping by Air: US: Add $5.00 for 1ˢᵗ book, plus $3.00 for each additional book. **Shipping International: Add $9.00 for 1ˢᵗ book, plus $5.00 for each additional book. USPS – **Media Mail** [6-10 days] 1 copy: $3.97, additional books: $1.97 each. USPS - **Priority Mail** (2-3 days) 1 copy: $6.47, additional books: $2.97 each.]

Payment: Check _____ Credit Card _____:
_____ Visa _____ MasterCard _____ AMEX

Card Number: _____

Name on Card: _____ **Exp Date:** _____

CPSIA information can be obtained
at www.ICGtesting.com
Printed in the USA
FSOW01n2020010218
44111FS